Global Tourism

Series Editor: Cara Acred

Volume 294

Independence Educational Publishers

First published by Independence Educational Publishers

The Studio, High Green

Great Shelford

Cambridge CB22 5EG

England

© Independence 2016

Photocopy licence

The material in this book is protected by copyright. However, the
purchaser is free to make multiple copies of particular articles for instructional
purposes for immediate use within the purchasing institution.
Making copies of the entire book is not permitted.

ISBN-13: 9781861687302

Printed in Great Britain
Zenith Print Group

Contents

Introduction

Global Tourism is Volume 294 in the **ISSUES** series. The aim of the series is to offer current, diverse information about important issues in our world, from a UK perspective.

ABOUT GLOBAL TOURISM

In 2014 travel and tourism contributed US$2.4 trillion to the world's gross domestic product and employment. But how is tourism changing? This book looks at how travel changes everyday life, the reasons why people travel and tourism in the UK. It also explores global tourism and sustainable travel, considering how you can be a responsible tourist and, indeed, whether this is possible without giving up flying.

OUR SOURCES

Titles in the **ISSUES** series are designed to function as educational resource books, providing a balanced overview of a specific subject.

The information in our books is comprised of facts, articles and opinions from many different sources, including:

⇨ Newspaper reports and opinion pieces

⇨ Website factsheets

⇨ Magazine and journal articles

⇨ Statistics and surveys

⇨ Government reports

⇨ Literature from special interest groups

A NOTE ON CRITICAL EVALUATION

Because the information reprinted here is from a number of different sources, readers should bear in mind the origin of the text and whether the source is likely to have a particular bias when presenting information (or when conducting their research). It is hoped that, as you read about the many aspects of the issues explored in this book, you will critically evaluate the information presented.

It is important that you decide whether you are being presented with facts or opinions. Does the writer give a biased or unbiased report? If an opinion is being expressed, do you agree with the writer? Is there potential bias to the 'facts' or statistics behind an article?

ASSIGNMENTS

In the back of this book, you will find a selection of assignments designed to help you engage with the articles you have been reading and to explore your own opinions. Some tasks will take longer than others and there is a mixture of design, writing and research-based activities that you can complete alone or in a group.

FURTHER RESEARCH

At the end of each article we have listed its source and a website that you can visit if you would like to conduct your own research. Please remember to critically evaluate any sources that you consult and consider whether the information you are viewing is accurate and unbiased.

Useful weblinks

www.adventure-life.com

www.aef.org.uk

www.blueandgreentomorrow.com

www.charlieontravel.com

www.theconversation.com

www.theguardian.com

www.ibtimes.co.uk

www.icrtourism.org

www.IUCN.org

www.nomadasaurus.com

www.responsibletravel.com

www.sustainabletravel.org

www.telegraph.co.uk

www.thetraveltype.com

www.timetric.com

www.unep.org

www.visitbritain.org

www.wearesalt.org

www.wttc.org

Economic Impact of Travel & Tourism: 2015 Annual Update

An extract from the report by the World Travel & Tourism Council.

Travel and tourism's direct contribution to world gross domestic product (GDP) and employment in 2014 was US$2.4 trillion (2014 prices) and 105 million jobs, respectively.

Taking its wider impacts into account, travel and tourism's total contribution to the global economy in 2014 was US$7.6 trillion (2014 prices), which equates to 9.8% of total economy GDP in 2014.

2.1 million new jobs were generated directly in the sector in 2014, and in total 6.1 million new jobs were created as a result of total direct, indirect and induced activity.

The total contribution of travel and tourism to employment grew 2.3% in 2014, while the total GDP contribution grew 3.6%, faster than the wider economy in 2014 and registering positive growth for the 5th successive year. This is again evidence that travel and tourism is a key engine for continued global growth and job creation.

Direct travel and tourism GDP growth in 2014 exceeded wider economic GDP growth in two-thirds (123) of the 184 countries covered by the annual economic impact research. Examples of countries where travel and tourism outperformed the wider economy include Greece and Sri Lanka. Since 2007, travel and tourism has significantly outperformed the wider economy in countries like Singapore, South Korea, Thailand, Turkey and UAE.

At a global level, travel and tourism out-performed growth in the majority of leading sectors in 2014, including automotive, public services, retail, ICT, financial services, aerospace and extraction. Its performance was only bettered by a small selection of booming sectors like consumer electronics and machine tools.

In total, travel and tourism supported 277 million jobs in 2014, 1 in 11 of the world's total.

Global performance 2014

⇨ 2014 proved to be yet another successful year for the travel and tourism sector off the back of a modestly stronger economic backdrop. World GDP growth increased from 2.3% in 2013 to 2.4% in 2014. The direct GDP contribution of travel and tourism grew by 3.5%, up from 3.4% in 2013.

⇨ The uplift in travel and tourism sector growth in 2014 was as predicted one year ago, though not by as much as forecast (4.3% forecast for 2014 versus the 3.5% outturn in 2014). World GDP growth of 2.4% was weaker than the 3.0% originally expected, with below expectations growth in Latin America, Japan, Mexico and Russia being the main sources for the world GDP downgrade. On top of this, other unexpected developments during 2014 contributed to weaker than otherwise travel and tourism performance: Ukraine-Russia conflict, Ebola in West Africa and political instability in Thailand. Countries like Syria and Libya remained highly unstable in 2014 and terror attacks in Nigeria and Kenya increased.

⇨ During a year of particular exchange rate volatility when the US dollar appreciated against the majority of currencies, visitor exports still grew by a robust 4.1%, outpacing growth in domestic tourism spending of 3.1%. International tourist arrivals increased by 4.7%, the fifth year in a row growth has exceeded 4%.

⇨ Various sector indicators support the view that travel and tourism performance was robust in 2014. Hotel performance was strong with higher occupancy rates and average daily rates in almost all regions. International air passenger demand grew by around 6%, measured in terms of revenue passenger kilometres, up from growth of 5.4% in 2013. Continued additions to seat capacity and expansion of routes, allied to some downward pressure on air fares from lower oil prices, should ensure that further growth in international air travel materialises in 2015.

- All major components of travel and tourism recorded growth in 2014, as did all world regions. Business and leisure spending grew by 3.4%, while travel and tourism investment increased by 3.9%. But in most cases growth was weaker than predicted one year ago in line with weaker than anticipated macroeconomic performance. Business spending growth was downgraded by more than leisure spending. Like last year, part of this may be attributed to continued efforts by Chinese authorities to clamp down on corruption by reducing business travel expenses on government-related business.

- South Asia, led by India, and the Middle East, were the fastest growing regions globally in terms of travel and tourism's total contribution to GDP. Europe's growth was weakest but its performance is improving. In terms of visitor exports, Europe out-performed North America in 2014 and is forecast to continue to do so in the medium-term given the strength of the US dollar. With the exception of parts of Asia where there has been a notable economic slowdown in recent years, such as in China, and Latin America where domestic economic weaknesses abound, all major regions recorded faster growth in travel and tourism's total contribution to GDP in 2014 compared to 2013.

- Africa's travel and tourism performance in 2014 picked up, despite the negative impact of Ebola on the sector in the parts of Africa directly and indirectly affected. Africa's improved performance was driven by stronger than expected performance in recovering Egypt and international growth in other major destination markets. The one exception is Kenya where terror attacks and travel warnings have impacted negatively on inbound tourism.

- Visitor exports growth in 2014, in real terms, was fastest in the Middle East and Africa, but slowed in Asia from 8.1% in 2013 to 4.4% in 2014. Political instability and the declaration of martial law in Thailand was a major explanatory factor for South East Asia's slowdown. A number of sub-regions enjoyed visitor exports growth around or well in excess of 5%, which in many cases was also above expectations: South Asia, Latin America, North Africa, Middle East, North East Asia, Oceania and Sub-Saharan Africa (even with Ebola). Japan and South Korea continue to benefit hugely from strong outbound spending growth from China and 2014 was no different.

- There were a number of smaller country 'hotspots' for growth in 2014, like Armenia, Oman, Qatar and Sri Lanka, which grew even stronger in percentage terms than bigger, fast growth markets like China, India, Indonesia, South Korea and Turkey.

- It is important, however, to set growth in a single year in the context of longer-term trends, especially given the sometimes volatile nature of international tourism flows. Thailand, despite its difficulties in 2014, has still experienced a 55% real increase in visitor exports since 2007. In contrast, visitor exports in Egypt, which improved in 2014, remain 20% lower than pre-Arab Spring levels, and 50% down on 2008 levels before the onset of the global recession and eurozone crisis.

Outlook 2015

- World total travel and tourism GDP growth of 3.7% will be stronger, again, than wider economy growth of 2.9%, exceeding wider economy GDP growth in over half of the 184 countries covered by the WTTC annual economic impact research. The sector's growth is forecast to again outperform growth in the majority of leading sectors in 2015 with

only consumer electronics and aerospace forecast to have significantly stronger growth.

⇨ Domestic travel and tourism spending growth is forecast to rise from 3.1% in 2014 to 3.7% in 2015, with global travel and tourism investment also rising from 3.9% to 4.8%. But world visitor exports growth is forecast to temporarily slow in 2015 from 4.1% to 2.8%, before returning to growth of +4% in 2016 and beyond and outpacing domestic spending growth.

⇨ The slowdown in visitor exports growth in 2015 is in line with a similar slowdown in world trade growth, weaker travel fares growth (linked to lower oil prices and travel fares), a sharp fall in Russian outbound visitor spending (the world's 5th largest outbound market) and the strength of the US dollar/ relative weakness of other currencies. But beyond 2015, visitor exports will continue to be driven by the appetite for travel beyond national borders, and the megatrend of an expanding middle-class, particularly from emerging markets.

⇨ The sharp fall in oil prices, which roughly halved in the second half of 2014 and into early 2015, is forecast to have a significant impact on oil exporting and net importing economies. It will also have knock-on impacts to exchange rates (where currencies are not pegged to the US dollar) and outbound tourism spending. Growth of oil-exporting economies like Saudi Arabia and UAE has been downgraded, even with OPEC's decision to maintain production levels. Russia is predicted to have a deep recession with GDP contracting by 6% on account of lower oil prices, sanctions, higher inflation from a substantially weakened rouble and the effects of the ongoing Ukraine-Russia conflict. Latin America's major economies, Brazil and Argentina, are again expected to struggle in 2015 with their growth downgraded

from one year ago. Based on these developments, travel and tourism GDP growth in 2015 has been revised down for the Middle East, Latin America and Russia. Russian outbound spending is forecast to fall by a third in 2015 which will impact negatively on destinations within Europe, such as Turkey and Montenegro, and markets as far apart as the US, UAE and Thailand.

⇨ Lower oil prices will benefit net oil importing economies and this is already being felt through falling inflation which is boosting real disposable incomes and consumer purchasing power. India and the UK's GDP growth forecasts for 2015 have been upgraded, while the US economy is expected to pick up with GDP growth of 3.3% in 2015. On the downside for the US, its economic strength will also be reflected in the strength of the US dollar, which is forecast to appreciate against all major currencies including the yen, euro and sterling. This will lead to slower growth in US visitor exports and faster growth in outbound spending in 2015, with Mexico, Canada and other major US outbound travel destinations set to benefit.

⇨ We expect travel and tourism in 2015 to generate in the region of 7.2 million new jobs in total, with 2.1 million new jobs directly created within the sector. This represents growth rates of 2.6% and 2.0%, respectively.

⇨ All major regions are forecast to enjoy both travel and tourism GDP and employment growth in 2015, assuming no unforeseen events, such as major natural disasters, significant escalation of conflict and sanctions, terrorism attacks or any reversal of the relative political stability. Travel and tourism growth is expected to continue to recover in Europe and North Africa, and pick up in South East Asia following Thailand's difficulties in 2014.

Trends to look out for over the next ten years include:

⇨ The prospect that China will overtake the US in terms of travel and tourism investment – but remain second behind the US in terms of travel and tourism total GDP, direct GDP, domestic spending and visitor exports.

⇨ UK, Mexico, India, Indonesia, Thailand, Myanmar and Montenegro will make noticeable moves up the global league table for total travel and tourism GDP.

⇨ China will move up two places to 2nd for visitor exports, overtaking Spain and France, with Thailand moving up six places to 4th, overtaking France, Germany and the UK.

⇨ China, US, Germany and the UK will retain the top four spots by 2025 for outbound spending (in that same order). Although approximately half of Chinese outbound spend today is to Hong Kong and Macau – adjusting for this in 2014 would shift its ranking today down to 3rd behind the US and Germany.

⇨ Singapore, Hong Kong, India, Indonesia, Malaysia, Qatar, Saudi Arabia, South Korea and Taiwan, will make noticeable moves up the global league table for outbound spending.

March 2015

⇨ *Economic Impact of Travel & Tourism 2015 Annual Update – Summary* by World Travel & Tourism Council is licensed under a Creative Commons Attribution-NoDerivatives 4.0 International Licence. Based on work at www.wttc.org/ research/economic-research/ economic-impact-analysis/.

Who's a tourist? How a culture of travel is changing everyday life

THE CONVERSATION

An article from The Conversation.

By Susanne Becken, Professor of Sustainable Tourism and Director Griffith Institute for Tourism, Griffith University

Every year, on 27 September, the global tourism community celebrates World Tourism Day. This year's theme is about community development and how tourism can contribute to empowering people and improve socio-economic conditions in local communities.

But who are the people who might visit "communities" and what does it mean – these days – to be a tourist?

There are many tourist stereotypes – an overweight Westerner in shorts with a camera dangling around their neck, or maybe a trekking-shoed backpacker hanging out in the Himalayas. Many people think of 'tourism' and 'holidays' as distinct times of the year when the family travels to the seaside or the mountains.

World Tourism Day is an opportunity to discuss how much more encompassing the phenomenon of tourism is than most people might think.

What is a tourist?

People are more often a 'tourist' than they realise. The United Nations World Tourism Organization broadly defines a tourist as anyone travelling away from home for more than one night and less than one year. So, mobility is at the core of tourism.

In Australia, for example, in 2013 75.8 million people travelled domestically for an overnight trip – spending 283 million visitor nights and $51.5 billion.

Reasons for travel are manifold and not restricted to holidays, which makes up only 47% of all domestic trips in Australia. Other reasons include participation in sport events, visiting a friend or relative, or business meetings.

Some of the most-visited destinations in the world are not related to leisure but to other purposes. For example, pilgrimage tourism to Mecca (Saudi Arabia) triples the population from its normal two million during the Hajj period every year.

Travel, work and leisure: what's the difference?

Tourists are not what they used to be. One of the most pervasive changes in the structure of modern life is the crumbling divide between the spheres of work and life. This is no more obvious than in relation to travel. Let me test the readers of *The Conversation*: who is checking their work emails while on holiday?

A recent survey undertaken in the US showed that 44.8% of respondents check their work email at least once a day outside work hours. Further, 29.8% of respondents use their work email for personal purposes.

Post-modern thinkers have long pointed to processes where work becomes leisure and leisure cannot be separated from work any more. Ever-increasing mobility means the tourist and the non-tourist become more and more alike.

The classic work-leisure divide becomes particularly fluid for those who frequently engage in travel, for example to attend business meetings or conferences. Conferences are often held at interesting locations, inviting longer stays and recreational activities not only for participants but also for spouses and family.

Further, city business hotels increasingly resemble tourist resorts: both have extensive recreational facilities such as swimming pools and spas, multiple restaurants and often shopping opportunities (e.g. Marina Bay Sands, Singapore). And, of course, they offer Internet access – to be connected to both work and private 'business'.

Understanding how people negotiate this liquidity while travelling provides interesting insights into much broader societal changes in terms of how people organise their lives.

For some entrepreneurial destinations these trends have provided an opportunity; namely the designation of so-called dead zones – areas where no mobile phone and no Internet access are available. Here the tourist can fully immerse in the real locality of their stay.

Fear of missing out

The perceived need to connect virtually to 'friends' (e.g. on Facebook) and colleagues has attracted substantial psychological research interest, with new terms being coined such as FOMO (fear of missing out) addiction, or Internet addiction disorder.

A recent Facebook survey found that this social media outlet owes much of its popularity to travel – 42% of stories shared related to travel. The motivations for engaging in extensive social media use and implications for tourism marketing are an active area of tourism research.

Thus, understanding why and what people share while travelling (i.e. away from loved ones, but possibly earning important 'social status' points) might provide important insights into wider questions of social networks and identity formation, especially among younger people.

Tourism and emigration

The increasingly global nature of networks has been discussed in detail by sociologist John Urry and others. They note the growing interconnectedness between tourism and migration, where families are spread over the globe and (cheap) air travel enables social networks to connect regularly.

As a result, for many people local communities have given way to global communities, with important implications for people's 'sense of place' and resilience. The global nature of personal networks extends to business relationships where the degree to which one is globally connected determines one's 'network capital'.

Urry also noted that mobility has become a differentiation factor between the 'haves' and 'have nots', with a small elite of hypermobile 'connectors'. Thus travel and

Intention to holiday overseas has risen in the UK for the third year in a row

80%
2015

78%
2014

Source: Holiday Trends 2015, BDRC Continental

tourism sit at the core of a potentially new structure of leaders and influential decision makers.

The global 'share economy'

Engaging in this global community of tourists is not restricted to those who travel actively. The so-called share economy, where people rent out their private homes (e.g. AirBnB), share taxi rides or dinners, has brought tourism right into the living rooms of those who wish to engage with people who they may not meet otherwise.

Potentially this parallel 'tourism industry' provides a unique opportunity for bringing people together and achieving peace through tourism. A whole new area for research travellers, 'guests and hosts' and their economic impacts, is emerging.

In a nutshell, tourism is much more than the service industry it is usually recognised for, both in practice and as a field of academic enquiry. Tourism and the evolving nature of travellers provide important insights into societal changes, challenges and opportunities. Engaging with tourism and travel also provides us with an excellent opportunity to better understand trends that might foster or impede sustainable development more broadly.

26 September 2014

⇨ The above information is reprinted with kind permission from *The Conversation*. Please visit www.theconversation.com for further information.

Reasons why people travel abroad

Travel is huge. According to the World Tourism Barometer there were over 1.1 billion international tourist arrivals in 2014. Significantly more than my wife or I can count on our fingers. To understand these nomads we Googled the reason why people like travel.

Dazed by 1.57 billion web results we exhumed the reasons by slogging through individual blog comments and travel forums. Again, thank you commenters; we love you and we used you. We grouped people's reasons for travelling abroad into six categories.

This is why people love to travel:

32% – People and culture

Curiosity about how others live is the foremost reason people travel.

Learning not to point with chopsticks, and eating the Australian witchetty grub or Icelandic puffin heart. Yum yum. Traditions entice the web-commenting traveller to go abroad.

Learning at home: what a chore, what a bore. Intrepid travellers want to climb over ruins and give history meaning. They are overseas to chat up the waitress in her own language.

24% – Perspective

Gaining outlook is the second most popular reason why people travel abroad.

While abroad, vacationers realise how messed up their priorities are. Bhutan has developed a Gross National Happiness measure for the lives of its citizens, which sounds nice. Meanwhile in Canada, workers feel guilty about wanting the vacation time just to visit Bhutan. Two different perspectives on what's important.

At home the news makes people fear the world. But savvy travellers know the media is skewing their perspective, so they leave home to correct it. People are travelling to form their own opinions.

14% – Adventure

Escaping from an ordinary life provides motivation to travel.

Grey cloth walls, grey suit-wearing colleagues and grey attitudes towards work. Breaking the routine is the reason why nine to five workers are travelling abroad. And when they arrive their inner Vin Diesel breaks out to go jet boating, mountain trekking, or bungee jumping.

Excitement is why people like to travel. Crossing the road in Vietnam, taking public transport in Zambia or scrumming in a Chinese queue gets the tourist blood pumping.

11% – Personal growth

People travel because it makes them better.

Do you remember *How Stella Got Her Groove Back* or *Eat Pray Love*? Sure the transformation was all in these ladies' minds, but travelling abroad did support their personal development.

Internet commenters are using travel to discover their strengths and weaknesses. Overcoming challenges, and growing because of it, is my particular favourite reason for travelling.

7% – Earth's beauty

The world is one sexy place and seeing it all is why people travel.

National Geographic-level photo-graphers armed with posh cameras fail to capture the emotion of the Grand Canyon. So tourists flock to Earth's stunning landscapes to experience Mother Nature for themselves. Then they buy t-shirts and mini-doughnuts.

Funny that the people who live next to natural wonders often fail to appreciate them.

12% – Other reasons

With a billion tourists each year, Internet forums are filthy with distinctive travel motives.

Not popular enough to make our cut: the love of planning, romance, relaxing on a beach, sex, being anonymous, partying, having a story to tell, and travelling just to say you've been there.

Information exclusions

It's doubtful that anyone only has one reason why they like to travel. Yet when prompted on the Internet, commenters could narrow their motives down. Our infographic represents the most prevalent reasons genuine people listed when commenting on blogs or in travel forums.

To keep our data pure we set a few rules. We ignored the opinion of anyone who spoke for more than themselves. Starting a comment with "People like to travel because…" guaranteed exclusion from our tally. We also ignored the 'lost bloggers'.

Lost bloggers are the few who haven't realised that public forums are not their soapbox. A detailed response is nice, but that doesn't mean you should promote your blog by copying an entire 500-word post into a forum. Bonus to those who pasted irrelevant photos along with their extensive responses. Too bad your opinion didn't make our cut either.

23 February 2015

⇨ The above information is reprinted with kind permission from The Travel Type. Please visit www.thetraveltype.com for further information.

The countries that rely most on your money

Tourism accounts for half the GDP of some countries, with the Maldives, the Bahamas and Aruba among the most dependent.

By Lizzie Porter

The world's island nations are typically the most reliant on income from tourism, along with destinations traditionally popular with British tourists, such as Thailand.

According to 2014 data from the World Travel & Tourism Council (WTTC), nine of the ten countries that rely most heavily on tourism are islands, including the Maldives and the Seychelles in the Indian Ocean, the British Virgin Islands, the Bahamas, Aruba and Anguilla in the Caribbean.

Macau – a special administrative region of China – relies more heavily than any other place, with 44 per cent of its Gross Domestic Product (GDP) stemming from the tourism and travel industries. The actual figure was $26.6 billion.

The British Virgin Islands – a British Overseas Territory – relies on the trade for a third of its wealth.

The value of tourism to the Maldivian economy last year was $1.03 billion – or 41.5 per cent of GDP.

Although absolute figures for travel and tourism's value are highest in other countries, including China ($263 billion), and the USA ($458 billion), they rank lower on this index because other industries generate even more wealth.

On the other hand, some countries have expressed the wish to attract more visitors, and the amount they spend, as other parts of their economies become less valuable in the long term. Oman, on the Arabian Peninsula, has earmarked tourism as an alternative to the oil industry on which it relies.

The majority of the data was sourced from the WTTC, and is based on the direct contribution made by the travel and tourism industries to each country's GDP in US dollars in 2014.

No data is available for many countries in Africa with unstable political situations, such as Eritrea, Somalia, and South Sudan. Figures for Afghanistan come from the World Bank and are based on receipts from international tourism in 2013, and its GDP from the same year.

The figure of less than one per cent for Tajikistan comes from the academic text *Nationalism and Identity Construction in Central Asia: Dimensions, Dynamics, and Directions* by Mariya Y. Omelicheva. The author writes that the country is currently trying to widen its potential, particularly with Turkmenistan.

According to the WTTC data, countries with little reliance on tourism as part of GDP include Chad and Suriname: tourism makes up just 1.1 per cent of total income in each.

17 September 2015

⇨ The above information is reprinted with kind permission from *The Telegraph*. Please visit www.telegraph.co.uk for further information.

Which countries travel the most?

Who are the most adventurous when it comes to travelling? A new study from Timetric ranks the world's most well-travelled countries.

⇨ Scandinavia is the world's most well-travelled region with Finland, Sweden, Denmark and Norway all being in the top five.

⇨ Finland tops the chart with the average Finn travelling 7.5 times a year.

⇨ The US is the largest domestic tourism market in the world. However, international travel is very limited with only one out of five Americans going abroad in 2013.

⇨ Mexico ranks surprisingly high, performing better than all of the BRIC countries.

Scandinavians are world's most well-travelled

According to Timetric's new data, Scandinavians travel the most, with the four Nordic countries all in the top five. The Finns top the chart with an average of 7.5 trips per person a year, followed by Sweden (6), Denmark (5.3) and Norway (5.2). According to Arnie van Groesen, travel and tourism analyst at Timetric, the reason

why Scandies travel so much comes down to money, weather and holiday traditions: "People in Scandinavia can afford more trips due to high incomes and relatively low unemployment rates. Cost of living is relatively expensive in Scandinavian countries, meaning that if they go abroad they'll often get more value for money. The weather conditions make them attracted to less severe conditions in the southern part of the world, such as the Spanish beaches." Furthermore, lots of Scandinavian people own second holiday homes and love to spend time in these so called "summer houses" in the country or by the sea. The Norwegians make two international trips per year on average, which is the highest in Europe.

The US is the world's largest domestic tourism market

The average American takes 6.7 trips a year. The large majority of these are domestic trips, making the US the largest domestic tourism market in the world in volume terms. International travel is very limited. Only one out of five Americans make an international trip a year and less than half of Americans own a passport. According to van Groesen, "going abroad is costly and the US is such a vast country it doesn't lack of things to see and do". Visiting friends and family is the main reason for domestic trips, as many Americans are living in a different state than where they grew up making it natural for them to travel back multiple times a year, with Thanksgiving and Christmas being peak periods. Another thing worth a note is travelling culture and the amount of time spent abroad. According to

van Groesen, many Americans, and other more excluded parts of the world, such as Australia, prefer to take longer and fewer trips abroad. Another reason why Americans prefer domestic trips is because of the low number of holidays. The Americans don't have any minimum rights of paid holidays and are often not allowed to take all their holidays at once. Across Europe, employers are entitled to an average minimum of 22 days paid holidays in 2013, excluding the number of public holidays.

Other countries worth a note

Hong Kong is the sixth most well-travelled country in the world. Although domestic tourism is almost nonexistent (0.03), the average Hongkongese takes 4.3 outbound trips a year, 74% of these to China. Mexico ranks surprisingly high, performing better than all the BRIC countries, especially domestic tourism, is very popular with 1.7 domestic trips a year. The total numbers for the BRIC countries are impressive, however the ratios show that there is still room for growth. Although China has the highest amount of total outbound trips (97.3 million trips in 2013), their ratio is very low: the majority of the Chinese population don't take international trips at all. Those who do, however, travel frequently. As a result of the shear size of the country, the number of outbound trips is deemed to be equally high.

9 October 2014

⇨ The above information is reprinted with kind permission from Timetric. Please visit www.timetric.com for further information.

Revitalise UK coastline to boost local economies

A new report from the New Economics Foundation marks the launch of a UK-wide initiative to deliver stronger economies for UK coastal communities and restore the health of the marine environment:

⇨ Good jobs and environmental sustainability are linked: improved management of our coastal and marine assets will create new, good jobs and boost struggling communities. NEF analysis shows that better management of UK fish stocks could create 4,922 new jobs

⇨ Coastal environments can support more than tourism: a healthy coast will have benefits for key coastal industries including renewable energy and fisheries and the well being of local communities

⇨ Transformation is already underway: case studies show innovative and sustainable approaches are already taking place across the UK – from innovative coastal management to sustainable business

⇨ Coastal actors from across the UK are already on board:

the Blue New Deal project will unite environmental goals with those of local communities and entrepreneurs.

The absence of social and environmental goals in key coastal and marine industries over the years has placed undue pressure on coastal economies, communities and the environment.

The Blue New Deal initiative, led by the New Economics Foundation (NEF), calls for a transformation of our approach to managing the UK's wealth of marine assets. The project will show how coastal areas can be revitalised to deliver good jobs and economic sustainability for coastal communities in the future.

Fernanda Balata, Project Lead, Coastal and Marine Environment, New Economics Foundation:

"As an island nation, the UK has access to a considerable wealth of natural resources. But our failure to properly manage them has told a story of unfulfilled potential – fewer jobs, lower revenues, unnecessary public costs, and unsustainable coastal economies. We want to deliver more and better jobs for coastal communities and the

marine environment plays a key role to help achieve that".

"Over the next year, we will work with actors across the UK to identify solutions and practical measures to improve the health of our marine and coastal ecosystems to address these challenges. There are great examples of innovative and sustainable approaches already happening around the UK coast – we need to put in place the incentives and policies to encourage action on a national scale."

Howard Wood, Chair and Co-Founder, COAST (Community of Arran Seabed Trust):

"The COAST initiative on the Isle of Arran is built around the concept that if the marine environment thrives, then everyone dependent on it will too. The Lamlash Bay No Take Zone is recovering well and this success is expected to have a positive effect on the surrounding waters, benefiting scallop divers and creelers that work within the newly created South Arran MPA. It also helps generate many tens of thousands of pounds for the local economy.

"The need to restore marine habitats and properly manage these ecosystems for the benefit of society and the economy is not unique to The Clyde. What's really exciting is that other groups across the country are waking up to the huge potential of our marine environment. The Blue New Deal is a welcome initiative to build on and strengthen this momentum."

The Blue New Deal identifies five key policy areas that offer the opportunity to respond to the different socio-economic and environmental challenges that the UK's coastal communities currently face. These include sustainable fisheries and aquaculture, innovative coastal management, renewable energy, responsible tourism, and re-connecting people with nature.

Over the next year, NEF will work with several partners – from local councils and national government departments, to entrepreneurs and industry representatives – to develop a nationwide action plan.

There are several examples of regional approaches that are already working across the UK. From investment in renewable energy to innovative management of our coastal environment, the following projects demonstrate that it is possible to create more jobs and support sustainable business through a healthier marine environment.

Innovative coastal management – Medmerry Realignment Scheme, West Sussex, Southeast England – innovative coastal defence has saved £300,000 in taxpayers' money each year and enabled year-round business opportunities by protecting environment and town infrastructure from flooding.

Renewable energy – Tidal Energy Ltd, Pembrokeshire, Southwest Wales – new tidal energy initiative to create new jobs and power 10,000 homes by 2017.

Marine conservation – COAST (Community of Arran Seabed Trust) Isle of Arran, Firth of Clyde, Scotland – community-led project promoting better protection of the marine environment to the benefit of people and the economy.

Sustainable business – The Venus Company, multiple locations, Southwest England – thriving chain of beachside cafes putting environmental and social considerations at heart to create sustainable employment.

30 June 2015

⇨ The above information is reprinted with kind permission from the New Economics Foundation (NEF). Please visit www.neweconomics.org for further information.

New plan to drive tourists beyond London

Government will boost tourism across the UK through new five-point plan.

The Prime Minister today announced the Government's new Five Point Plan to boost tourism right across the UK -–spreading the benefits of one of our fastest growing sectors beyond the capital, helping to create jobs and rebalance the economy.

A new inter-ministerial group will be formed to co-ordinate and align action across government to ensure that we have the right infrastructure in place to make it easy for visitors to discover the best of what this country has to offer.

The group, headed by the Culture Secretary John Whittingdale, and including ministers from across government, including the Department for Communities and Local Government, BIS, DEFRA, Home Office, and the Foreign and Commonwealth Office, will focus on five key areas:

⇨ A better co-ordinated sector: the sector is too fragmented – we want to see local attractions and tourism organisations collaborating to grow the sector for everyone not competing.

⇨ Skills and jobs: driving and retaining talent in the sector to encourage growth

⇨ Common sense regulation: reforming regulation sensibly to drive competition and improve the tourism offer for visitors.

⇨ Transport: forging innovative links between the transport and tourism sectors to help visitors travel outside of the capital.

⇨ An improved welcome: delivering a world-class welcome at the Border.

Ministers from the Scottish, Welsh and Northern Ireland Governments are also invited to join the group when relevant.

The Prime Minister has also announced:

⇨ A £1-million 'Rail for Tourism innovation' competition, which will call for ideas to transform the travel experience for visitors to the UK and make exploring the UK by rail more attractive to tourists. The competition will be run by the RSSB's Future Railways Programme, and winners will receive funding to develop their ideas and carry out trials.

59% of British people say that the coast is the most appealing Wellness destination in the Uk

Source: Holiday Trends 2015, BDRC Continental

The plan will build upon the enormous success of the 2011 tourism strategy, which culminated in a record year for overseas visitors in 2014 and now sees the industry contribute £60 billion to the UK economy a year. By opening up new experiences to tourists, we can build on this and ensure more visitors travel outside London and experience the very best of Britain.

Continuing his visit to the South West today the Prime Minister, David Cameron, said:

"Millions of overseas tourists visit the UK every year and most take in the sights of London. But Britain has so much more to offer, from the Cornish Riviera to the Scottish Highlands and everything in between.

"For many areas tourism is a key industry bringing jobs, growth and security for working people. Tourism supports almost one in ten jobs in the UK and we want to rebalance the economy to make sure this boost is felt right across the country."

Culture Secretary, John Whittingdale, said:

"Tourism is a vital industry that brings jobs and growth to local economies across Britain. There are so many world-class things to see and do in the UK, and we need to make sure visitors are experiencing as many of them as possible.

"I am delighted to chair this new group which will put tourism at the heart of government and help to ensure that every part of the UK benefits by co-ordinating action across government. We want every visitor to the UK, whether from home or abroad, to have a brilliant experience and shout about it, encouraging even more tourists to choose Britain."

The plan and funding announced today is in addition to new funds announced in March to boost tourism in both the South-West and the North. The £5-million fund for the South-West will position the area as a must-see destination, generating an additional £60 million in additional visitor spending, creating up to 1,000 jobs and incentivising local partners to work together on improving the experience for visitors to the region. It will also be used to promote the South West in the USA and encourage greater connectivity to the region from the United States.

There is a £10-million fund to support northern destinations to attract international visitors from around the world and ensure the North is on the map as a top tourist destination - a key part of our plan to build a 'Northern Powerhouse'.

Tourism has grown quickly since the Government's previous tourism strategy in 2011. The direct contribution of the tourism sector to the economy in 2014 was almost £60 billion – up a fifth since 2010. Last year, international visitors spent a record £21.8 billion in local economies across the country, with nearly every region seeing a rise in visitor numbers or spend. In 2013, it was estimated that 9% of jobs in the UK were in tourism-related industries and jobs in the sector were growing at almost double the rate of other industries.

Simon Vincent OBE, EVP and President, EMEA at Hilton Worldwide said:

Hilton Worldwide strongly supports the tourism plan announced by the Prime Minister, placing an industry that contributes one in ten jobs and 9% of GDP at the heart of the Government's agenda.

"The travel, tourism and hospitality sectors are growing twice as fast as the rest of the UK economy and at Hilton Worldwide we have opened 50 hotels in the UK since 2007 alone, employing more than 12,000 people. Building on the success of the Tourism Industry Council, we look forward to working with ministers from all government departments to help deliver the new tourism plan."

17 July 2015

⇨ The above information is reprinted with kind permission from the Department for Culture, Media & Sport, the Prime Minister's Office, 10 Downing Street, the Department for Transport, The Rt Hon. David Cameron MP and others.

Structure of tourism in Britain

Britain's tourism industry is a dynamic affiliation of public and private sector organisations including small- to medium-size enterprises (SMEs); international private businesses (e.g. airlines or large hotel chains), as well as Destination Management Organisations (DMOs) at local and regional level.

Each of the countries within the British Isles also has its own national tourist board which works closely with us. Britain also has a wealth of tourism industry and trade associations.

VisitBritain is a non-departmental public body, funded by the Department for Culture, Media & Sport (DCMS) through a grant-in-aid (GIA).

The Secretary of State of DCMS is John Whittingdale, who is responsible to the UK Parliament for VisitBritain's activities. The Minister with responsibility for tourism is Tracey Crouch. The UK Government sets the overall strategy, policy and objectives for tourism.

VisitBritain is the strategic body for inbound tourism to Britain, responsible for the international tourism promotion of Britain and its nations and regions. Take a look at the about us section to find out more about our role, activity and priorities.

England

VisitEngland is the national tourist board for England and is legally accountable to the board and Accounting Officer of VisitBritain and has its own CEO and board. It is responsible for the development of standout tourism products through the management of an English tourism challenge fund and domestic marketing.

Tourism is a devolved matter. Scotland, Wales and Northern Ireland all have independent tourist boards. The Mayor of London also has a promotional agency – London & Partners. VisitBritain works closely with all of these organisations.

Scotland

VisitScotland is the national tourism organisation for Scotland. It has a strategic role as the public sector agency providing leadership and direction for the development of Scottish tourism to get the maximum economic benefit for Scotland. It exists to support the development of the tourism industry in Scotland and to market Scotland as a quality destination.

Wales

Visit Wales is the Welsh Assembly Government's tourism team, within the Department for Heritage. Visit Wales has taken over the functions of the former Wales Tourist Board (WTB), with responsibility for the promotion and development of tourism in Wales.

London

London & Partners is the official promotional agency for London, attracting and delivering value to businesses, students and visitors. It is a not-for-profit public private partnership, funded by the Mayor of London and a network of commercial partners. Their remit is to drive leisure and business visitors as well as bidding to secure major events in London.

Northern Ireland

The Northern Ireland Tourist Board is part of the Department of Enterprise Trade and Investment. Its primary objective is to promote Northern Ireland as a tourist destination.

The Channel Islands

Jersey and Guernsey both have Crown Dependency status but are not part of the United Kingdom. The tourism body on these islands are a department of their respective governments.

There are also a wide number or regional Destination Management Organisations and local authorities with responsibility for tourism to their specific area.

⇨ The above information is reprinted with kind permission from VisitBritain. Please visit www.visitbritain.org for further information.

© VisitBritain 2015

How does the UK economy affect where the British go on holiday?

Changes to holiday destinations 2007–2013.

There is some evidence to suggest that UK residents changed their travel behaviour during the years of the economic downturn in 2008–09, by choosing to take holidays within Great Britain rather than abroad. This has been referred to as the "Rise of the 'Staycation'", but are we now seeing the fall? This analysis looks at data on holiday visits from 2007 to 2013. A holiday visit is defined as a visit to a destination for holiday purposes that includes at least one overnight stay.

Increase in number of UK residents going on holiday abroad between 2012 and 2013

Between 2008 and 2009 there was a major change in the holiday visits of UK residents, with a 16% fall in visits abroad according to the International Passenger Survey. At the same time the Great Britain Tourism Survey which looks at GB

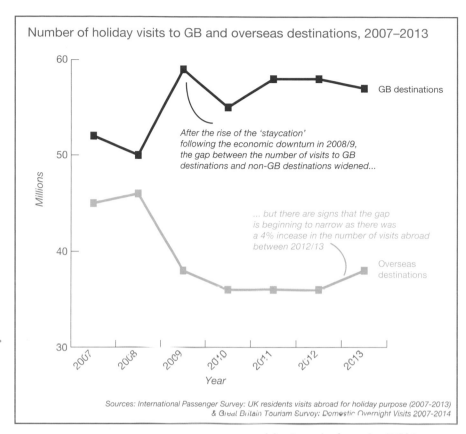

Number of holiday visits to GB and overseas destinations, 2007–2013

GB destinations

After the rise of the 'staycation' following the economic downturn in 2008/9, the gap between the number of visits to GB destinations and non-GB destinations widened...

... but there are signs that the gap is beginning to narrow as there was a 4% increase in the number of visits abroad between 2012/13

Overseas destinations

Millions

Year

Sources: International Passenger Survey: UK residents visits abroad for holiday purpose (2007-2013) & Great Britain Tourism Survey: Domestic Overnight Visits 2007-2014

residents only, found a 17% increase in holiday visits to destinations in Great Britain. These figures widened the gap between visits to GB and non-GB destinations.

The most recent figures show that this gap may be starting to narrow; there was a 4% increase in the number of UK residents holidaying abroad between 2012 and 2013, alongside a 1.3% decrease in visits to GB destinations. When more data becomes available for 2014 it may become clearer if tourists are once again travelling abroad or if the staycation is here to stay.

1 August 2014

⇨ The above information is reprinted with kind permission from the Office for National Statistics. Please visit www.ons. gov.uk for further information.

Responsible tourism

Chapter 2

Tourism's three main impact areas

Negative impacts from tourism occur when the level of visitor use is greater than the environment's ability to cope with this use within the acceptable limits of change. Uncontrolled conventional tourism poses potential threats to many natural areas around the world. It can put enormous pressure on an area and lead to impacts such as soil erosion, increased pollution, discharges into the sea, natural habitat loss, increased pressure on endangered species and heightened vulnerability to forest fires. It often puts a strain on water resources, and it can force local populations to compete for the use of critical resources.

Depletion of natural resources

Tourism development can put pressure on natural resources when it increases consumption in areas where resources are already scarce.

Water resources

Water, and especially fresh water, is one of the most critical natural resources. The tourism industry generally overuses water resources for hotels, swimming pools, golf courses and personal use of water by tourists. This can result in water shortages and degradation of water supplies, as well as generating a greater volume of waste water.

In dryer regions like the Mediterranean, the issue of water scarcity is of particular concern. Because of the hot climate and the tendency of tourists to consume more water when on holiday than they do at home, the amount used can run up to 440 litres a day. This is almost double what the inhabitants of an average Spanish city use.

Golf course maintenance can also deplete fresh water resources. In recent years golf tourism has increased in popularity and the number of golf courses has grown rapidly. Golf courses require an enormous amount of water every day and, as with other causes of excessive extraction of water, this can result in water scarcity. If the water comes from wells, overpumping can cause saline intrusion into groundwater. Golf resorts are more and more often situated in or near protected areas or areas where resources are limited, exacerbating their impacts.

An average golf course in a tropical country such as Thailand needs 1,500kg of chemical fertilisers, pesticides and herbicides per year and uses as much water as 60,000 rural villagers.

Source: Tourism Concern

Local resources

Tourism can create great pressure on local resources like energy, food, and other raw materials that may already be in short supply. Greater extraction and transport of these resources exacerbates the physical impacts associated with their exploitation. Because of the seasonal character of the industry, many destinations have ten times more inhabitants in the high season as in the low season. A high demand is placed upon these resources to meet the high expectations tourists often have (proper heating, hot water, etc.).

Land degradation

Important land resources include minerals, fossil fuels, fertile soil, forests, wetland and wildlife. Increased construction of tourism and recreational facilities has increased the pressure on these resources and

on scenic landscapes. Direct impact on natural resources, both renewable and nonrenewable, in the provision of tourist facilities can be caused by the use of land for accommodation and other infrastructure provision, and the use of building materials.

Forests often suffer negative impacts of tourism in the form of deforestation caused by fuel wood collection and land clearing. For example, one trekking tourist in Nepal – and area already suffering the effects of deforestation – can use four to five kilogrammes of wood a day.

Pollution

Tourism can cause the same forms of pollution as any other industry: air emissions, noise, solid waste and littering, releases of sewage, oil and chemicals, even architectural/visual pollution.

Air pollution and noise

Transport by air, road and rail is continuously increasing in response to the rising number of tourists and their greater mobility. To give an indication, the ICAO reported that the number of international air passengers worldwide rose from 88 million in 1972 to 344 million in 1994. One consequence of this increase in air transport is that tourism now accounts for more than 60% of air travel and is therefore responsible for an important share of air emissions. One study estimated that a single transatlantic return flight emits almost half the CO_2 emissions produced by all other sources (lighting, heating, car use, etc.) consumed by an average person yearly. (Mayer Hillman, Town & Country Planning magazine, September 1996. Source: MFOE.)

Transport emissions and emissions from energy production and use are linked to acid rain, global warming and photochemical pollution. Air pollution from tourist transportation has impacts on the global level, especially from carbon dioxide (CO2) emissions related to transportation energy use. And it can contribute to severe local air pollution. Some of these impacts are quite specific to tourist activities. For example, especially in very hot or cold countries, tour buses often leave their motors running for hours while the tourists go out for an excursion because they want to return to a comfortably air-conditioned bus.

Noise pollution from airplanes, cars and buses, as well as recreational vehicles such as snowmobiles and jet skis, is an ever-growing problem of modern life. In addition to causing annoyance, stress, and even hearing loss for humans, it causes distress to wildlife, especially in sensitive areas. For instance, noise generated by snowmobiles can cause animals to alter their natural activity patterns.

Solid waste and littering

In areas with high concentrations of tourist activities and appealing natural attractions, waste disposal is a serious problem and improper disposal can be a major despoiler of the natural environment – rivers, scenic areas, and roadsides. For example, cruise ships in the Caribbean are estimated to produce more than 70,000 tons of waste each year. Today some cruise lines are actively working to reduce waste-related impacts. Solid waste and littering can degrade the physical appearance of the water and shoreline and cause the death of marine animals.

In mountain areas, trekking tourists generate a great deal of waste. Tourists on expedition leave behind their garbage, oxygen cylinders and even camping equipment. Such practices degrade the environment with all the detritus typical of the developed world, in remote areas that have few garbage collection or disposal facilities. Some trails in the Peruvian Andes and in Nepal frequently visited by tourists have been nicknamed 'Coca-Cola trail' and 'Toilet paper trail'.

Sewage

Construction of hotels, recreation and other facilities often leads to increased sewage pollution. Wastewater has polluted seas and lakes surrounding tourist attractions, damaging the flora and fauna. Sewage runoff causes serious damage to coral reefs because it stimulates the growth of algae, which cover the filter-feeding corals, hindering their ability to survive. Changes in salinity and siltation can have wide-ranging impacts on coastal environments. And sewage pollution can threaten the health of humans and animals.

Aesthetic pollution

Often tourism fails to integrate its structures with the natural features and indigenous architecture of the destination. Large, dominating resorts of disparate design can look out of place in any natural environment and may clash with the indigenous structural design.

A lack of land-use planning and building regulations in many destinations has facilitated sprawling developments along coastlines, valleys and scenic routes. The sprawl includes tourism facilities themselves and supporting infrastructure such as roads, employee housing, parking, service areas and waste disposal.

Physical impacts

Attractive landscape sites, such as sandy beaches, lakes, riversides, and mountain tops and slopes, are often transitional zones, characterised by species-rich ecosystems. Typical physical impacts include the degradation of such ecosystems.

An ecosystem is a geographic area including all the living organisms (people, plants, animals and microorganisms), their physical surroundings (such as soil, water and air), and the natural cycles that sustain them. The ecosystems most threatened with degradation are ecologically fragile areas such as alpine regions, rain forests, wetlands, mangroves, coral reefs and sea grass beds. The threats to and pressures on these ecosystems are often severe because such places are very attractive to both tourists and developers.

In industrial countries, mass tourism and recreation are now fast overtaking the extractive industries as the largest threat to mountain communities and environments. Since 1945, visits to the ten most popular mountainous national parks in the United States have increased 12-fold. In the European Alps, tourism now exceeds 100 million visitor-days. Every year in the Indian Himalaya, more than 250,000 Hindu pilgrims, 25,000 trekkers and 75 mountaineering expeditions climb to the sacred source of the Ganges River, the Gangotri Glacier. They deplete local forests for firewood, trample riparian vegetation and strew litter. Even worse, this tourism frequently induces poorly planned, land-intensive development.

Source: People & the Planet

Physical impacts are caused not only by tourism-related land clearing and construction, but by continuing tourist activities and long-term changes in local economies and ecologies.

Physical impacts of tourism development

Construction activities and infrastructure development

The development of tourism facilities such as accommodation, water supplies, restaurants and recreation facilities can involve sand mining, beach and sand dune erosion, soil erosion and extensive paving. In addition, road and airport construction can lead to land degradation and loss of wildlife habitats and deterioration of scenery.

In Yosemite National Park (US), for instance, the number of roads and facilities have been increased to keep pace with the growing visitor numbers and to supply amenities, infrastructure and parking lots for all these tourists. These actions have caused habitat loss in the park and are accompanied by various forms of pollution including air pollution from automobile emissions; the Sierra Club has reported "smog so thick that Yosemite Valley could not be seen from airplanes". This occasional smog is harmful to all species and vegetation inside the Park.

Source: Trade and Environment Database

Deforestation and intensified or unsustainable use of land

Construction of ski resort accommodation and facilities frequently requires clearing forested land. Coastal wetlands are often drained and filled due to lack of more suitable sites for construction of tourism facilities and infrastructure. These activities can cause severe disturbance and erosion of the local ecosystem, even destruction in the long term.

Marina development

Development of marinas and breakwaters can cause changes in currents and coastlines. Furthermore, extraction of building materials such as sand affects coral reefs, mangroves and hinterland forests, leading to erosion and destruction of habitats. In the Philippines and the Maldives, dynamiting and mining of coral for resort building materials has damaged fragile coral reefs and depleted the fisheries that sustain local people and attract tourists.

Overbuilding and extensive paving of shorelines can result in destruction of habitats and disruption of land-sea connections (such as sea-turtle nesting spots). Coral reefs are especially fragile marine ecosystems and are suffering worldwide from reef-based tourism developments. Evidence suggests a variety of impacts to coral result from shoreline development, increased sediments in the water, trampling by tourists and divers, ship groundings, pollution from sewage, overfishing, and fishing with poisons and explosives that destroy coral habitat.

Physical impacts from tourist activities

Trampling

Tourists using the same trail over and over again trample the vegetation and soil, eventually causing damage that can lead to loss of biodiversity and other impacts. Such damage can be even more extensive when visitors frequently stray off established trails.

Trampling impacts on vegetation	Trampling impacts on soil
Breakage and bruising of stems	Loss of organic matter
Reduced plant vigour	Reduction in soil macro porosity
Reduced regeneration	Decrease in air and water permeability
Loss of ground cover	Increase in run off
Change in species composition	Accelerated erosion
Source: University of Idaho	

Anchoring and other marine activities

In marine areas (around coastal waters, reefs, beach and shoreline, offshore waters, uplands and lagoons) many tourist activities occur in or around fragile ecosystems. Anchoring, snorkelling, sport fishing and scuba diving, yachting and cruising are some of the activities that can cause direct degradation of marine ecosystems such as coral reefs, and subsequent impacts on coastal protection and fisheries.

Alteration of ecosystems by tourist activities

Habitat can be degraded by tourism leisure activities. For example, wildlife viewing can bring about stress for the animals and alter their natural behaviour when tourists come too close. Safaris and wildlife watching activities have a degrading effect on habitat as they often are accompanied by the noise and commotion created by tourists as they chase wild animals in their trucks and aircraft. This puts high pressure on animal habits and behaviours and tends to bring about behavioural changes. In some cases, as in Kenya, it has led to animals becoming so disturbed that at times they neglect their young or fail to mate.

⇨ The above information is reprinted with kind permission from the United Nations Environment Programme. Please visit www.unep.org for further information.

What is sustainable tourism?

One of the best definitions of sustainable tourism is that written by the United Nations World Tourism Organization, which addresses what sustainable tourism actually should be doing.

Sustainable tourism should

1. Make optimal use of environmental resources that constitute a key element in tourism development, maintaining essential ecological processes and helping to conserve natural heritage and biodiversity.

2. Respect the socio-cultural authenticity of host communities, conserve their built and living cultural heritage and traditional values, and contribute to inter-cultural understanding and tolerance.

3. Ensure viable, long-term economic operations, providing socio-economic benefits to all stakeholders that are fairly distributed, including stable employment and income-earning opportunities and social services to host communities, which contribute to poverty alleviation in those areas.

Sustainable tourism development requires the informed participation of all relevant stakeholders, as well as strong political leadership to ensure wide participation and consensus building.

Achieving sustainable tourism is a continuous process and it requires constant monitoring of impacts, introducing the necessary preventive and/or corrective measures whenever necessary.

Sustainable tourism should also maintain a high level of tourist satisfaction and ensure a meaningful experience to the tourists, raising their awareness about sustainability issues and promoting sustainable tourism practices amongst them.

What's the most effective way of raising awareness of sustainable tourism to travellers and holidaymakers?

Through word of mouth. One of the greatest avenues by which people not only learn about other destinations and activities, but actually 'trust' the source, is through word of mouth. Getting sustainable tourism on social media sites, having folks discuss these products on blogs, National Geographic and other forms of popular media really can be effective.

What are the benefits of making the global travel and tourism industries sustainable? What are the consequences of not doing this?

To me, the obvious benefits are that we actually conserve the wonders of the world and the special places of the world that make our planet environmentally and culturally diverse. We can also improve the quality of people's lives, who are ultimately very dependent on healthy and diverse ecosystems – for human survival. As the leading economic driver on our planet, tourism has a unique opportunity to influence how the world operates. Sustaining places sustains us as human beings. Without a healthy planet where industries operate, sustaining ecosystem services, where human rights are respected, where quality of life is improved, we really cannot exist long term.

Is it contradictory to use aeroplanes on a sustainable holiday?

Air travel is a super highway in the sky. We know the many benefits tourism can bring to regions that have limited development alternatives; therefore, we must continue to look at reducing emissions, better technology and improved methods for air travel. Countries such as Costa Rica are looking at ways to improve offsets and create carbon neutral experiences for those travelling to their shores, because of their reliance on international tourism. There are no easy solutions, and improvements must be made. Weighing it all out is an important research problem. Would a destination be better off with no international travellers? I don't think we have the answers just yet.

What is the real economic case for sustainable tourism?

We reached just over one billion travellers last year. Hence, over a billion opportunities to effect positive change. In some economies, income earned from tourism 'leaks' out, and as a result does not benefit local communities. When this happens, the economic benefits are realised in other places. So the economic case for sustainable tourism is that the income generated must recycle into the local community. When this happens, infrastructure is improved, people benefit directly in ancillary businesses, employment improves, and ultimately poverty is reduced.

One argument around the future of tourism is that we simply need to have fewer holidays, particularly to the most far-flung places on Earth, to be truly sustainable. To what extent do you agree?

I am not sure I agree and would like to continue to pursue this idea through evidence-based research – real evidence one way or the other. The alternatives for some destinations reliant on tourism are not great. I think we need to continue to explore what other development opportunities are available for destinations or locales. Fewer holidays are not necessarily the answer; most likely it is more important to look at population growth and what we consume overall. Travel is not necessarily the 'criminal'. It is more likely that increased population with increased demands on the world's resources will be the cause of our demise. We need to learn to live within our means, use resources wisely, conserve the ecosystem services upon which human life really depends, develop in a way that does not create a mess for some other location, etc. There are larger issues at stake here, and travelling may not be the worst of it all. However, we must learn to develop travel experiences in a sustainable way, and as an industry we are clearly not all on the same page just yet.

What are the key sustainable tourism trends for the next decade?

Great and difficult question. This is really anybody's guess, but given the current conditions, people are going to increase their own knowledge of sustainable products, and therefore become more educated consumers as evidenced in online programmes. Companies are going to seek sustainable verification and operations to reduce risk, improve marketing appeal to consumers and reduce costs overall. The planet will continue to be under siege, and therefore, sustainability in all sectors of society will be a must; because of human reliance on ecosystem services, industries will continue to look towards efficiency, low-impact improvements to their operations and increasing quality of life attributes, which will increase in importance Products will be designed to increase connection to the environment, and enhance quality of life at the destination level. Sustainable tourism is moving from a product focus to a destination level focus – sustainability in tourism will focus on supply chains, community and region level sustainability.

15 July 2015

⇨ The above information is reprinted with kind permission from Blue & Green Tomorrow. Please visit www.blueandgreentomorrow.com for further information.

Can you be a sustainable tourist without giving up flying?

An article from The Conversation.

By Morgan Saletta, Doctoral Candidate and Graduate TA in History and Philosophy of Science, University of Melbourne

Australians love to travel. About nine million Australians travelled overseas last year, 60% of them on holiday. For most tourists, sustainable development and climate change were probably not high on their list of concerns. But increasing numbers of travellers are concerned about these issues.

> **"So is it possible to enjoy an overseas holiday without contributing to catastrophic climate change? Will our enjoyment of a remote tropical beach literally submerge it under rising sea levels?"**

Is sustainable tourism possible when tourism accounts for about 5% of global greenhouse gas emissions? If the tourism sector were a country, it would be the fifth-largest greenhouse emitter in the world.

By far the largest source of these emissions is transport, particularly air travel. If the current growth trend continues, these emissions could triple within 30 years.

On the other hand, tourism is incredibly important for local development. Indeed, it offers the only sustainable means of economic development for many developing countries. The UN World Tourism Organization says that tourism will be important in reaching the Millennium Development Goals, which include ensuring environmental sustainability and eliminating extreme poverty.

Exactly how the tourism industry can best help to meet these goals is a matter of debate. However, it seems clear that tourism can make a positive contribution to conservation efforts around the world as well as boosting local economies, although you do have to pump out greenhouse gases to get there.

To travel or not to travel, that is the question

What options does the environmentally concerned tourist have? Is the only responsible action to restrict holidays to places that can be reached by foot, bike or train? This is certainly not impossible, but it seems unlikely that enough people would be willing to do it to deliver much of an impact. And even if they did, they would deprive many developing countries of the economic and environmental benefits of tourism.

As the UN Environment Programme points out, tourism is one of the main ways to pay for nature conservation and protection. For example, the Orangutan Foundation project in Indonesia's Tanjung Puting National Park receives US$45,000 (A$51,000) every year from wildlife travel agency Steppes Discovery, a member of the Tour Operators Initiative for Sustainable Tourism Development. This money pays for rangers, the care of orphaned orangutans, and helps fund the park.

So is it possible to enjoy an overseas holiday without contributing to catastrophic climate change? Will our enjoyment of a remote tropical beach literally submerge it under rising sea levels? Is there a balance between the environmental costs of tourism and its benefits? Sustainable tourism arguably means working out what this balance is, and then ensuring we stay on the right side of it.

Carbon offsets: atoning for sins of emission?

Reducing emissions growth projected in a 'business as usual' scenario requires changes both in consumer behaviour and in the way the tourism industry is structured.

Carbon-offset schemes are not universally supported, and can be confusingly complex. It is important to understand that there are uncertainties involved in such offset schemes. Because they aim merely to offset emissions rather than reduce them, some people reject these schemes altogether as an option. Some even portray the notion of offsetting as a modern-day indulgence for climate sins.

Some of the criticisms are valid. But purists miss an important point: many activities that are vital to global development goals are unlikely ever to be emissions-free. Tourism is one such activity.

Carbon-offset schemes and the standards by which they are accredited certainly need monitoring and regulation. Ultimately this will need to be done within the framework of a global climate treaty. They are, however, a positive example of business opportunities generated by the demand for low-carbon tourism options.

For the individual tourist, offsetting is increasingly easy and cheap. According to the Qantas calculator, offsetting a round-trip from Melbourne to Los Angeles only costs about A$25 at present. Flights within Australia can be offset for as little as the price of a cup of coffee.

Other tourism activities can be offset too – rental car firm Europcar, for instance, offers offsets purchased through carbon forestry company Greenfleet.

Other companies offering offsets in Australia include Climate Friendly, Carbon Planet, and Carbon Neutral. These firms engage in many types of offset projects including forestry, wind power, and others. Our Planet Travel recommends that consumers look into the types of projects an offset scheme uses, to ensure it is one they support.

Forestry projects, in particular, have attracted a lot of attention. It is generally accepted that forest growth can store carbon dioxide, and an analysis of forest carbon sink projects found that this approach can be useful in meeting emissions-reduction targets. However, these projects come with inherent uncertainties: if a forest burns, for example, the stored carbon is re-emitted.

Of course, climate change itself may exacerbate the risk of such fires. On the other hand, timber harvested from forestry projects is safe from bushfires and could still be counted towards the offset total, because it still contains much of the carbon from the tree. All of these different factors will need to be studied carefully, preferably at an international level as part of an agreed climate treaty.

A guilt-free pleasure?

Given that offsets seem to be a way of having one's cake and eating it too, these schemes should appeal to tourists. By offsetting, they can enjoy their holiday and contribute to global development while at the same time atoning for their sins of emission. Unfortunately, according to Qantas, only 5% of air travellers currently choose to offset.

"For the individual tourist, offsetting is increasingly easy and cheap"

Sadly, this is an area where consumer choice may not be best and responsible governments as well as corporations need to take the lead. Ecotours, for example, often bundle carbon offsets into their price. It can only be hoped that airlines will follow suit.

Ultimately, however, what's required is a clear global framework for reducing emissions, in which offsets can play a part. We need, in other words, an international climate agreement. The devil, as always, will be in the details.

24 October 2014

⇨ The above information is reprinted with kind permission from *The Conversation*. Please visit www.theconversation.com for further information.

© 2010–2015, The Conversation Trust (UK)

Eco-friendly accommodation options and how to find them

A blog post from Charlie on Travel.

If like me you are feverish with wanderlust but also keen to be as eco-friendly as possible while travelling, then you might want to look into making eco-friendly accommodation choices. You don't need to spend a fortune to be an eco-friendly traveller, but making eco-conscious choices often takes a reasonable amount of research.

Unfortunately, it can be all too easy to end up staying in a hotel or resort that has a negative impact on the environment without even realising it. Collectively, hotels are guilty of excessive energy consumption, unnecessary overuse of water and poor waste management. From bigger issues like building in areas where construction ruins the environment down to the little things like pumping out air conditioning and washing bed linen daily, hotels can leave a huge carbon footprint.

Instead of choosing a large resort or a chain hotel, instead look for alternative, eco-friendly accommodation such as camping, home stays, local guesthouses or at least an eco-hotel that does its bit for the environment and the local people.

What makes accommodation eco-friendly?

If you're on the search for eco-friendly accommodation, then you need to know what kind of things to look out for. Of course, no accommodation is perfect but if they can fulfil at least some of the criteria then they're on the right track. According to the EU Ecolabel for accommodation, the accommodation should be trying to lessen its impact on the environment by:

⇨ Limiting energy consumption

⇨ Limiting water consumption

⇨ Reducing waste production

⇨ Using renewable energy

⇨ Promoting environmental education

Sometimes finding out all of this information about a hotel can be a challenge, but more often than not the hotel's website will be proud to show off its commitment to the environment and the local community. As a general rule of thumb, smaller or locally run accommodation will have a lower impact than big hotels or resorts irrelevant of any claims about green practices.

One point to be aware of is the issue with greenwashing – when companies or hotels describe something as more responsible or 'eco-friendly' than it actually is. It can be hard to differentiate between genuinely committed and sustainable accommodation options and ones that are dressing up their business to make money off the back of the green movement. There aren't any laws to stop businesses using 'green' or 'eco' labels, so you've just got to read between the lines.

Eco-hotels, Eco-lodges and Eco-retreats

There are loads of cool eco-hotels around the world boasting everything from self-contained pods that reduce carbon emissions to off-the-grid nature retreats that grow all their own veg. While some are inevitably more sustainable than others, we've found that most of the time the eco-hotels, lodges and retreats are genuinely trying to lower their impact on the environment.

By far the most admirable example of an eco-lodge which we've come across is La Kukula in Costa Rica which is powered by renewable energy and uses clever design and passive cooling to avoid the

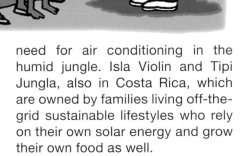

need for air conditioning in the humid jungle. Isla Violin and Tipi Jungla, also in Costa Rica, which are owned by families living off-the-grid sustainable lifestyles who rely on their own solar energy and grow their own food as well.

Staying local and eco-friendly accommodation in cities

Most travellers spend their time in the capital and other big cities and don't want to be without an Internet connection for long periods of time, but there are still responsible accommodation options. In some countries, finding locally run accommodation can be really easy. For example, in Nicaragua the cities on the main tourist routes, such as Leon and Granada, are relatively small places and there are lots of local people running guesthouses at reasonable prices.

We've found that in larger cities, where finding local and eco-friendly accommodation is more of a challenge, it can be worth checking out Airbnb to see if there are any places to rent in a non-touristic neighbourhood or in a local's house. When we were in Bangkok recently, we stayed in a cool little city-based homestay with a really accommodating couple and it was a way better experience than any of the larger hotels could provide.

Home-stays and house sitting

Another eco-friendly accommodation option is to forget about hotels and guesthouses altogether and instead go in search of alternative accommodation with local families and communities. Many homestays involve volunteering or language learning components that also support the local communities by contributing to the local economy. By staying with a local family, you'll also use far fewer resources than you would do in any hotel.

House sitting may not be your first thought when it comes to eco-friendly accommodation but by travelling slowly and staying in one place for a longer period of time you're lessening your carbon footprint. By opting out of staying in hotels that were built for tourists you're also decreasing the demand for them.

Other eco-friendly accommodation alternatives

My list is by no means a definitive one when it comes to looking for eco-friendly accommodation. There are also plenty of opportunities for more outdoor-style accommodation such as camping, staying in tipis and yurts, and local huts.

In the past, Luke and I have really loved using Couchsurfing as well as a way to find shared accommodation and meet with locals, and we've met hosts through Facebook and on Craigslist as well. Although we've only had positive experiences of meeting people via online networks, we always recommend exercising caution and chatting to people on Skype or meeting for coffee first of all.

Charlie is a slow traveller from the UK who writes about responsible and sustainable travel. She travels, writes and house sits her way around the world with her partner, Luke. For them, travel is a lifestyle, not just a holiday.

13 July 2015

⇨ The above information is reprinted with kind permission from Charlie on Travel. Please visit www.charlieontravel.com for further information.

Five ways to give back to travel destinations you care about

Travel can be exhilarating, relaxing, inspiring or obligatory. So whether you take to the road for work or pleasure, travel can provide an opportunity for you to contribute to the well-being of the places you care most about. Here's how...

1) Eat local

Help bolster local economies by opting for locally sourced food and locally owned restaurants. For example, choose family-owned restaurants in lieu of fast food burgers or pizza chains. When you eat local, you're not only supporting local restaurants but neighbourhood farmers and fishermen. Not only that, enjoying the local cuisine is often a very satisfying way of savouring the local culture.

2) Shop local

Unless you're in China, avoid buying items manufactured there. Choose souvenirs for sale in local markets and artisan co-ops. Support businesses that are giving back to communities. Check out Visit.org, an online marketplace for tours and activities run by local nonprofits.

3) Leave a legacy

As visitor numbers increase and resources for natural and cultural protection dwindle, traveller philanthropy programmes are becoming increasingly popular and important. Travel Oregon and Torres del Paine are two examples of these types of initiatives. Read more about how a small grant from visitor donations helped The Human Access Project secure over $300,000 from the city of Portland, Oregon to improve access to the Willamette River coastline.

4) Share

A spectacular vista, an intriguing encounter, a meditative moment. Share your experiences on Facebook, Twitter, Instagram – keep friends and family in the know. Tell them who you've met, what you've learned and how you've felt. That way, you'll inspire others to travel in support of people and the planet.

5) Support our work

Donate today and support our work in destinations around the world. From creating new job opportunities for indigenous communities in Suriname to fruit tree planting in St. Kitts, your donation can make a significant difference in the lives of people who depend on travel and tourism.

6 August 2015

⇨ The above information is reprinted with kind permission from Sustainable Travel International. Please visit www.sustainabletravel.org for further information.

Sustainable tourism in protected areas can be critical for their survival, says new IUCN report

Increasing the number of visitors to protected areas can be an effective tool for conservation and community development, provided well-functioning management systems are in place, according to a new report unveiled today at the IUCN World Parks Congress taking place in Sydney, Australia.

Highlighting a global collection of case studies from Machu Picchu in Peru to the Damaraland Camp in Namibia, the IUCN report, *Tourism and Visitor Management in Protected Areas: Guidelines for Sustainability*, includes contributions from more than 50 experts from 23 countries and territories, and examples from over 45 countries around the world.

"Unlike other industries and human-driven activities, tourism in protected areas can be a strong positive force – increasing a sense of stewardship and revenues that are vital for the long-term protection of these important conservation areas," said Dr Yu-Fai Leung, the chief editor of the report and member of the IUCN WCPA Tourism and Protected Areas Specialist Group. "By contrast, reduced visitor numbers to protected areas can signal a lack of political interest or public support. The guidelines provided in this report are intended to strengthen current visitor management systems, including measures on how best to protect these key natural and cultural assets."

International tourism is a trillion-dollar business, accounting for up to 9% of global GDP. The World Tourism Organization estimates that tourism is expected to continue to grow by 3.3% annually through 2030, generating one in 12 jobs globally. Protected areas, including National Parks and World Heritage Sites, are consistently the primary attraction for tourists interested in exploring natural areas and its wildlife across the world.

Governments, protected area agencies, tour operators, retailers and members of the local community can all benefit from tourism revenues and in some cases tourism enterprises directly support the protection or rehabilitation of key habitat areas.

For example, payments made by Wilderness Safaris – a private sector ecotourism company – for annual concession fees for ecotourism camps in Africa in 2014 totalled over $4.4 million, a substantial contribution to financing protected areas through tourism.

In contrast, the report finds that where visits to protected areas have dropped, such as in Canada, Japan and the United States, the parks have suffered from reduced political support and funding. For example, between 1994 and 2012, there was a 28.7% decrease in the number of visitors to national parks in Canada, which may have contributed to the government's 2012 decision to cut budget and staff to national parks.

The report recognizes that protected area managers are grappling with a number of challenges, including climate change, illegal wildlife trade, inadequate infrastructure and competing interests for natural resources. However, with proper management systems in place, an increase in visitors can generate much needed revenues from entrance fees, guided tours, accommodation and concessions, which in turn can be invested in conservation activities.

The report highlights the need to identify and evaluate the true costs and impacts of tourism in protected areas, in order to have a clear understanding of the opportunities and challenges related to the development of tourism in these areas.

"With international travel expected to rise, protected areas managers need to mitigate any negative impacts as a result of increased visits, but also identify new opportunities stemming from this potential demand that can provide revenue for conservation and the local economies. Innovative approaches and partnerships with the local communities, private enterprises and government are needed to help strike the balance in securing long-term support for these critical areas," concluded Anna Spenceley, co-editor of the report and Chair of the IUCN WCPA Tourism and Protected Areas Specialist Group.

About the report

Tourism and Visitor Management in Protected Areas: Guidelines for Sustainability was coordinated by Yu-Fai Leung, Anna Spenceley, Glen Hvenegaard and Ralf Buckley of the IUCN World Commission on Protected Areas' Tourism and Protected Areas Specialist Group. The report includes contributions from 54 experts from 23 countries and territories, and examples from 44 countries around the world. The report builds on existing literature, incorporating new research, theoretical frameworks, planning management strategies, case studies and recommendations. Project site: http://iucn.oscar.ncsu.edu.

14 November 2014

⇨ The above information is reprinted with kind permission from IUCN. Please visit www.IUCN.org for further information.

Thoughts on green travel

By Elizabeth Conway

Sustainable, Responsible, Green, Eco Tourism – I know it can be tough to get beyond these labels and into the meaning behind such abstracts. But here's a little help... traveller, Sarah Shelton, provides some direction and does a great job highlighting the sort of questions you should ask your travel company if you are looking at going green on your next adventure.

Green travel

Green travel, also called sustainable travel or ecotourism, focuses on vacations that minimise the impact on the local environment and culture. Good green travel companies emphasise sustainable practices over just maximising their bottom line. This can include recycling water, offsetting carbon emissions, and positively supporting the local culture.

Why travel green?

With over a billion people travelling internationally each year, there is an enormous environmental impact. And it includes more than just extra water and fuel. Unregulated tours overpopulated some areas, leaving wildlife areas trashed and crowded, marred with excessive roads. Neither tourists nor the native people benefit from these spoiled habitats. The essence of sustainable travel is to create an enjoyable vacation that benefits the locals but doesn't harm the land.

Finding green companies

Buyer beware: just because a company claims a green standard, doesn't make it so. Doing a little bit of legwork confirms that your travel dollars really are supporting sustainable travel. Here are four essential qualities that a good green travel company will possess:

Environmental impact: do they use small, less intrusive group sizes? Are they proactive in minimising their carbon footprint? Do they emphasise the 'Leave No Trace' principles in their trips? Companies that they partner with, like the local hotels, should also be geared toward conservation.

Cultural impact: it is important that your travel company shows respect for the local culture, and highlights their traditions. Not only is this beneficial to the native people, but it provides a more authentic trip for you.

Economical impact: do they support the local economy? Hotels, tours, and transportation companies owned locally are a few of the businesses they might work with. This gives you a more genuine experience, removing the sterile feel of a worldwide chain, and keeps more money in the local economy.

Certificates or memberships: there are a number of organisations that promote sustainable travel. For example, the International Ecotourism Society promotes environmental conservation throughout its worldwide network of members.

As an added bonus: does the company support local causes? Some go above and beyond good business practices to support organisations that focus on conservation or provide needed resources to local people.

Good green companies:

Adventure Life – This tour company offers tours to South and Central America destinations, as well as Antarctica tours and Expedition cruises. Highlighted by *National Geographic* as one of 'The Best Adventure Travel Companies (On Earth)', they pride themselves in offering excellent expeditions while maintaining a high quality of sustainable travel.

ResponsibleTravel.com offers one of the largest selections of ecofriendly travel, including luxury tours and safaris. Locations are available worldwide, and there are also a number of special interest trips to choose from.

WWF – The World Wildlife Fund has expanded its mission to include travel offerings. Specialised trips are available in many exotic locations, highlighting indigenous people and wildlife. As an added bonus, portions of the trips also benefit this amazing organisation.

Be a green traveller

Don't just pay to support ecotourism- join in! Help make your trip ecofriendly:

Leave No Trace: more than just a slogan, this simple message reminds us that we take nothing away but our trash and our photos.

Respect nature: wildlife should always be admired at a distance. Don't disrupt them or their habitat, and never try to feed them.

Respect locals: be sensitive to other cultures and their differences. The standard rule is to always ask before taking their photograph. Also, if you are going to take time to travel to their area, why not take a little time to learn a little of the language and native customs?

What you practise at home: remember all the tips you use on a daily basis? Recycle when you are able, take short showers to save on hot water, and use alternative transportation like walking and biking. While it is tempting to indulge, remember that you can still have a great experience and be responsible at the same time.

These are just a few of the things that you can do. Here are a few more tips:

Green travel can offer a new way to travel. Not just a good choice, it could be the adventure of a lifetime. Experience new cultures, see amazing wildlife, or just relax on the beach. Whichever you choose, green travel is the way to go.

Last edited, 13 May 2013

⇨ The above information is reprinted with kind permission from Adventure Life. Please visit www.adventure-life.com for further information.

Turtles and tourism

They may have outlived the mass-extinction of dinosaurs, but sea turtles face a new threat: tourism.

By Iris Knoop, Responsible Travel

Sea turtles have been around for millions of years. They migrate long distances around the world, feeding on anything from jellyfish to sea urchins and sea grasses, but always return to the same beach they were born on to lay their eggs. The female crawls ashore to lay up to 120 eggs, covers up the nest with sand using her flippers and returns to the sea, never to see her hatchlings.

The hatchlings will emerge from the nest in large groups and make a dash for the sea by following the light of the moon and stars reflecting in the sea. It is estimated that only around one in every 1,000 of them will reach maturity in about 20 years and they may grow over 80 years old.

The ever increasing demand from tourism for pristine, sandy beaches – often favoured by sea turtles – has been detrimental to turtle nesting habitats worldwide. This development, combined with increasing pollution and bycatch of turtles out at sea, not to mention locations where turtle meat and eggs are still considered a delicacy, has lead to a global decline of sea turtle populations.

Sun beds, hotels and people on or adjacent to the beach have reduced the space available for nesting. 'Beach cleaning' with heavy machinery, sand extraction and erosion have changed the sand consistency of many beaches and even destroyed nests.

These are just some of the problems – turtles are very shy and all this activity on the beach may prevent them laying and cause them to abort their eggs. Lights from developments and hotels disorientate the hatchlings and prevent them finding their way to the sea.

Fortunately, there are many organisations and individuals trying to reverse the decline. They are working hard to minimise detrimental effects, educate the public and provide hands-on conservation and protection measures. Anyone can help turtles

and the environment in general by being a conscientious traveller, supporting these organisations, or helping as a volunteer.

Why volunteer on a turtle project?

So it's clear that sea turtle conservation is important for the continuing survival of these species, but there are many other reasons why sea turtle volunteering can be so rewarding.

Yes, it will probably be hard work – traipsing along miles of beach at 5am in the morning looking for signs of the elusive turtle (there is no guarantee you will actually see one!), but knowing you're giving something back makes it all the more rewarding.

You'll learn about endangered species and their wider ecosystems, gain an understanding of the environmental field, get to know a different culture, contribute to turtle conservation and all that while meeting some great people! And aside from that, if you are lucky enough to have an encounter with this ancient mariner, it is a humbling experience and something that will stay with you forever.

Things you can do on your holiday

There are several things you can do to help while on holiday in a sea turtle nesting area:

⇨ Do not go on the beach at night – you may disturb a turtle trying to nest or step on a hatchling

⇨ Do not use torches or flashlights on the beach at night - it can distract hatchlings on their way to the sea. If you are staying near the beach, ensure your lights are turned off after dusk, or ask your hotel to.

⇨ Do not buy any turtle products

⇨ Clear your sunbed and umbrella off the beach at night and don't leave any litter. It can obstruct the mother or trap the hatchlings, and plastic bags can in the sea be mistaken by turtles for jellyfish and ingested.

⇨ The above information is reprinted with kind permission from Responsible Travel. Please visit www.responsibletravel.com for further information.

© Responsible Travel 2015

What is responsible tourism?

The contribution of responsible tourism

⇨ minimises negative economic, environmental and social impacts;

⇨ generates greater economic benefits for local people and enhances the well-being of host communities, improves working conditions and access to the industry;

⇨ involves local people in decisions that affect their lives and life chances;

⇨ makes positive contributions to the conservation of natural and cultural heritage, to the maintenance of the world's diversity;

⇨ provides more enjoyable experiences for tourists through more meaningful connections with local people, and a greater understanding of local cultural, social and environmental issues;

⇨ provides access for physically challenged people; and

⇨ is culturally sensitive, engenders respect between tourists and hosts, and builds local pride and confidence.

Taking responsibility for tourism

Responsible Tourism is about making "better places for people to live, and better places for people to visit" – the order of these two aspirations is critical. The characteristics of RT as defined in the Cape Town Declaration are very generic; it is for destinations and enterprises to determine their priorities in the light of the environmental and socio-cultural characteristics of the destination. Diversity, transparency and respect are core values.

All forms of tourism can be more responsible. Progress relies on "all stakeholders taking responsibility for creating better forms of tourism and realising these aspirations". Responsible Tourism relishes "the diversity of our world's cultures, habitats and species and the

wealth of our cultural and natural heritage" and therefore accepts "that responsible and sustainable tourism will be achieved in different ways in different places". One policy or set of criteria will not apply everywhere – nor should they. The Declaration emphasises that it is only at the local level, where tourists and locals interact, that tourism can be sustainably managed.

The Declaration called on "planning authorities, tourism businesses, tourists and local communities – to take responsibility for achieving sustainable tourism". Individuals in tourism businesses can make a big difference, but there is also a major role for government, particularly in destinations. Local and national governments need to shoulder their responsibilities: progress requires joined up government (UK) or a whole of government approach (South Africa). The language differs, but the imperative is the same: tourism can only be managed in destinations when the different agencies work together. The Cape Town Declaration recognised the importance of "transparent and auditable reporting of progress" and that benchmarking is essential to assess progress and to facilitate consumer choice. No simple label can serve this purpose.

In the next phase of RT development, we are likely to see more countries and destinations developing policies and implementation strategies and the development of RT audits of tour operations. The annual Responsible Tourism Awards (sponsored by Virgin Holidays, the *Daily Telegraph* and *Geographical magazine* and announced on World Responsible Tourism Day at World Travel Market each November) demonstrate the diversity and strength of the movement, but its very success has encouraged some unscrupulous companies to adopt the language but omit the practice.

Responsible tourism has become a movement. It's broad and diverse; there's a vanguard; there are laggards and hangers on; there's now a 'fringe' event each year at WTM on the night

before World Responsible Tourism Day. The movement remains relatively transparent, and there is debate and a ratchet effect as expectations rise – entries which won in 2004 wouldn't make the short list in 2009. But for the movement to continue to achieve change, we need rebellious tourists and rebellious locals, we need activists in destinations and tourism enterprises, and we need travellers and holidaymakers to hold the operators and accommodation providers to account. If a consumer is dissatisfied with the sustainable credentials of a property which relies on one of the ecolabels for its credibility, there's little that they can do – they have no contract with the label provider and therefore no redress. The explicit RT claims made by the operator or accommodation provider are part of the contract and redress can be sought.

What does it mean, to take responsibility?

There are two ways of thinking about responsibility. They are interdependent, but politically they are different. One strand can be characterised as accountability. Actions and consequences can be attributed to individuals or legal entities , who can be held accountable, and legally they are liable. Revealing the consequences of actions or inactions can also be used to raise awareness and elicit a response. Responsibility can be given in a rather limited legal sense, but the ICRT is more focussed on encouraging individuals to take responsibility – it is individuals who make the difference, individuals change the world.

This second strand is active. It is about responding to a perceived need. The work of the ICRT is predicated on 'respons-ability', focussed on enabling individuals to respond and to make a difference. This requires partnerships, a plurality of relationships, learning, praxis and critical reflection. The ICRT recruits students who are mid-career, who've had some experience of work and are looking to make change in the world. Our students have empathy, they have a strong sense of the 'other', they've travelled and they've seen the impacts of tourism in destination communities. They recognise interdependence and the responsibility which flows from that. They have the impetus to responsibility, they have or seek roles where they can exert agency. They require what Aristotle called *phronesis*, the ability to determine ends and to act in particular contexts. This requires prudence and a degree of maturity.

The ICRT leads a very public existence: our students arrive committed to RT and wanting to make a difference. They have shared aspirations and value sets around taking responsibility for the triple-bottom-line sustainability of tourism. Many of them will have spoken with one of our alumni or met us through a conference or consultancy; they will have read the Cape Town Declaration. They join us with high expectations that they will acquire the knowledge and skills to make a difference, they know that they should because they can. Opportunity imposes responsibility.

They seek really useful knowledge; they want to be equipped, enabled, to respond.

It's difficult to predict which of our alumni will make the biggest contribution in the real world – there is certainly no easy correlation with grades. To make change is to run a marathon, it's not a sprint. Stamina and perseverance, resilience, self-criticism, and the willingness after failure to try again, are essential. As Gramsci cautioned and demanded, "Pessimism of the Intellect, Optimism of the Will."

The ICRT is about change. It is committed. It is for RT. There's a shared commitment to the principles of the Cape Town Declaration – when alumni meet they have a lot in common. The alumni and current students, who will become alumni, share a broad commitment to using tourism to "create better places for people to live in, and better places for people to visit". There's plenty of debate about ends and means – and the relationship between them, but there is also a shared acceptance of the responsibility, and willingness to act, to make at least a small part of the world a better place. The curriculum

reflects this with a unit on Securing Change and a recurring focus on the application and generation of knowledge.

It's not enough simply to understand – it's also important to take responsibility and to act. Very few of our alumni pursue academic careers – they work in the industry, in local government, in conservation or archaeology, for consultancies, for newspapers and development banks, for UN agencies, alongside communities. They make a difference. The alumni are our most powerful recruitment mechanism. They are part of our approach to lifelong learning, through the network and by coming along to our conferences and alumni evenings held in London. The annual reunion on World Responsible Tourism Day brings together 70+ alumni, current students, associates and colleagues. When the mergers took place last year and TUI and Thomas Cook both established RT teams; we had, and still have, students in both teams working to advance the agenda.

In the class of 2001 the group decided that there needed to be a market place for RT, an awards programme and a Foundation. All three now exist, and more besides. ResponsibleTravel.com was launched in 2001, co-founded by myself and Justin Francis, a member of that class, although I sold my interest some years ago. RT.com prospers as the world's largest online travel agency for responsible holidays. The 21st-century equivalent of Fish Street, it employs a number of our alumni and has enabled the growth of many small businesses.

We hope you join us in our journey of taking responsibility for a more sustainable tourism.

⇨ The above information is reprinted with kind permission from the International Centre for Responsible Tourism. Please visit www.icrtourism.org for further information.

© International Centre for Responsible Tourism 2015

Responsible travel – you have the choice

To Our Friends,

Alesha and I created NOMADasaurus a little less than a year ago with the vision of promoting sustainable tourism and long-term travel. The 'sustainable tourism' part of our mission is based on our belief that, through the ways we travel, the regions we visit and the choices we make on how and where we spend our money, can have a positive impact on communities and families that are not as fortunate as ourselves. Another name for it is 'responsible travel'.

Travelling opens up the doors to a world that can be both incredibly rewarding and desperately unfortunate. While many of us back in the 'real world' are more concerned about which new shoes we are going to buy and whether it is time to upgrade our TV or not, there are tragic circumstances occurring every day that we are trained to ignore.

According to UN Water, 783 million people do not have access to clean water and almost 2.5 billion do not have access to adequate sanitation. six to eight million people die annually from the consequences of disasters and water-related diseases.

805 million people do not have enough food to lead a healthy and active life. 21,000 people die every day from hunger-related causes.

Please take a moment to think about how substantial those numbers are.

It is easy to ignore these stats and figures and instead focus on our own lives and the issues we have going on between ourselves, friends and family. It is the normal thing to do.

We are not here to say that the problems we face back in the 'first world' are not important. Of course, you must help yourself before you help others. But Alesha and I are travellers in a unique position to witness some of these 'foreign problems' first hand and we feel obligated to help out when and where we can. When it comes to responsible travel, we are huge advocators. Sustainable tourism is at the forefront of our thoughts and continues to fuel the fire inside us.

It is hard to say which charities need more assistance over others and who is more deserving of our help. Recently the ALS Ice Bucket Challenge went viral and raised many funds for a great cause, despite the questionable values of the company that received the donations. Everyone has their own idea of where they would like to see their money spent and everyone deserves that choice. In this one particular situation, 5,600 people are diagnosed with ALS every year. This is quite upsetting, I agree, and it is incredible that so much help has been given to those who are affected by this debilitating disease. Over $100 million and counting so far! But who suffers more?

The cause that Alesha and I feel the most passionate about is access to clean drinking water. The numbers mentioned above are pretty scary. I come from a place where I can bathe myself for hours in clean water, and now I am backpacking in a country where nearly half of the population does not have access to the same luxury just to survive. It is something we take for granted and is easy to ignore when we cannot see it with our own two eyes.

This is not a problem that is impossible to rectify.

Compared with the billions (and trillions) of dollars governments around the world are spending on war, imprisonment, immigration and unfortunately greedily pocketing themselves, not much is really needed to make a huge difference. It is estimated that as little as $10 billion would be required to provide clean drinking water to the entire population. Or just 1.2% of the world's military expenditure. Or just 15% of what the citizens of the US spends on alcohol and tobacco every year. Or less than what the Australian Government has committed to spend on some shiny new fighter jets.

Are our priorities really in the right place?

In Cambodia, where we are travelling right now, 20% of deaths of children under the age of five are caused by drinking dirty water. To us, this is unacceptable.

In a small effort to help combat this terrible situation, we have donated the funds required to build a water well in a rural village here in Cambodia. This post is not about big noting our pittance of a donation. It is not a means to justify our ideas of responsible travel and sustainable tourism. We do not consider ourselves heroes, or kings and queens of charity, pretending to save the world while I sit here writing on my Apple laptop. We do not have all the answers and indeed we are far from perfect ourselves. Simply put, this is something we felt obligated to do. The more we travel, the more we learn. This post is about promoting awareness.

If you are in a position to travel please think about how and where you spend your money. Choose responsible travel. Eating at corporate fast food chains and only staying in international hotels does little to see your hard-earned money make a positive impact on local communities. Avoiding developing or poor countries because of fear and being uninformed affects many people, yourself included.

How can you help? By buying food from the street vendors. Staying in locally-run guesthouses. Purchasing your supplies from small convenience stores in your destination instead of the market chains at home. Don't give money to children who ask but instead support an enterprise that works personally with these underprivileged kids.

Some restaurants, cafes, tour companies and other businesses work closely with communities and charities. Sometimes the prices they have for services and products are a little higher than you can get elsewhere. Step back and think about how that extra few dollars out of your own pocket can potentially help a worthwhile cause. These types of expenditures are worth paying more for.

If you have the time to volunteer with an organisation, be very careful about which one you choose. Do your research and ensure the skills you provide and the money you spend will be utilised properly. Don't do it for yourself, for a Facebook picture, to tell your friends back home how you 'saved the planet'. Do it for the planet and for its people. Responsible travel is the key.

Realise that donating a lump sum of money is not the only way to make a difference, although this is indeed worthwhile. All you need to do is make conscious decisions. If you are already travelling, or are planning on travelling, you can make a positive difference if you choose sustainable tourism. Even if just once on your journey you sacrifice a little bit of luxury to provide business or assistance to someone who needs it, you are helping the cause. If would like some more advice on the best

ways to do this, please contact us.

Life is about choices, but this only applies to those privileged enough to be born with these choices available to them. Not everyone has the luxury to be reading a travel blog on the Internet. To be dreaming about seeing the world. To be considering spending money on a holiday instead of scratching to see where the next meal is coming from. We are extremely lucky. Don't forget it, or take it for granted.

If you've made it this far, thank you very much for reading. If you agree, please share this around. If you have suggestions, comments or criticism please let us know. Open the discussion for better ideas on responsible travel. Promote awareness. Promote sustainable tourism.

If you are able to travel, travel responsibly. Make that choice and stick by it. Your actions can have a big impact.

"Be the change that you wish to see in the world." – Mahatma Ghandi

Much love,

Lesh and Jazza

NOMADasaurus

29 September 2014

Irresponsible tourism

When it is just wrong.

By Catherine Mack

Sadly, the tourism industry just gets things wrong sometimes and, at Responsible Travel, we strive to highlight the pitfalls of our desire to discover the world. Sometimes at any cost. Or else, carried away by our desire to have a much needed break, we just turn a blind eye to irresponsible tourism. This is also not helped by the fact that many travel companies and the travel media fail to highlight the serious issues and impacts of our travel on many destinations. Mass media coverage is given to abuses arising in fashion, food and forestry but holidays are often seen as sacrosanct. They are our time to escape the stresses of everyday life, and no one wants to be made feel guilty about travel or think of themselves as an irresponsible tourist.

The other issue is that travel media is often funded by the travel industry through complimentary trips to journalists, many of whom are therefore resistant to give negative coverage. There are always exceptions, but travel editors, in general, don't like

to shout about the dark sides of tourism. Not when a big tourist board, airline, all inclusive-holiday company or cruise multinational is about to spend thousands advertising on their website. We know this from first-hand experience, as we campaign against various detrimental activities in tourism, and gaining coverage in the travel press is always an uphill struggle. We're not bitter. We just know that the media, and other travel companies, can do better. Read more about this in our feature, *Is travel writing in the National Press truly independent or influenced by advertisers?*

The irresponsible travel round up

Our travel blacklist

Here are some of the no-no's of travel which we would like all tourists to be aware of, whether they are reading right on, red tops or rags of newspapers. Because we celebrate travel, we don't always want to give you the bad stories. We want to

stress that for every irresponsible way of doing things, there is nearly always an alternative – one that is just as exciting, adventurous, restful and fun as the dodgy one. Here, in alphabetical order, are some of our no-no's of travel. Please share with anyone you know who loves to travel and who is still turning a blind eye:

All-inclusive resorts

They might be a bargain and tough to resist, but the multinational, homogenous, fly-and-flop resorts are low on ethical cred and high on negative environmental and economic impact. According to UK charity Tourism Concern, few countries benefit directly from all-inclusive resorts, as the foreign owned tourism company owns the hotel, airline, ground transport and often excursion providers. For example, their recent research found that, in Turkey, only ten percent of tourist spend from all-inclusive holidays found its way into the regional economy, with even less reaching the immediate local area. Rather than condemning them all outright, at Responsible Travel we do believe that all-inclusive holiday companies have the potential to be a lot more responsible and that indeed, some are taking baby steps to doing so, by sourcing more food locally, or using local activity providers and so on. From a travel point of view, what most people don't know is that all-inclusives aren't always the cheapest way to holiday, if you just know where to look.

Canned hunting

Canned hunting is when animals such as lions are reared simply for the purpose of being hunted on privately owned reserves – this is to be avoided at all costs. It does nothing for the environment – or for local people. There are several canned hunting reserves in South Africa, and tourists should also be wary of the fact that some of these are also in the market for 'conservation volunteers'. Unwittingly, tourists turn up to count, care for and monitor animals, unaware that elsewhere on this massive, privately owned piece of land, the animals are then being hunted – for a fee of tens of thousands of pounds.

Alarm bells should ring any time volunteers are permitted to interact with wildlife – feeding, cuddling and petting them – as any truly wild creature (or one which is destined for release) should never become habituated. Irresponsible tourism at its most ironic and ignorant.

Captive animals

Animals that are kept in captivity have long been used as tourist attractions or for frivolous entertainment. Our best piece of advice is, in general, if it isn't in the wild, then it isn't where it ought to be. There are some sanctuaries or conservancies that are exceptions of course but, as a rule of thumb, if it is doing something that isn't natural, then the animal has been forced to do so in a way that is, in our opinion, unethical. Captive dolphins and whales are off the radar unethical, and you can read more about this in our 'Say no to Orca Circuses' campaign.

Elephant trekking, riding, washing and playing are not on our list of top things to do either, as you can see from our 'Elephants in tourism' guide, although we make some exceptions when it comes to creating conservation income in national parks that helps protect endangered species, such as tigers in India. However, the mistreatment of these wild animals to titillate tourists is not something we endorse in any way. Dancing bears or any performing animals really are dodgy, such as snake charmers and dancing monkeys in Morocco.

Child sex tourism

The use of children for prostitution is a reality in many countries, such as Thailand, Sri Lanka and Madagascar to name but a few. The harsh reality is that this is a huge growth area in tourism, with children being trafficked for this purpose, even though in most cases they don't realise that this is why they are being sent to a place, but think that they are going to do legitimate jobs. Although girls are sexually exploited, the UN states that it is young boys who face greater abuse by foreign sex offenders. Always report any suspect activities with regards to children to local authorities and, in particular, the tourism locations which are allowing it to happen. The Code (short for 'The Code of Conduct for the Protection of Children from Sexual Exploitation in Travel and Tourism') is an excellent point of contact for this purpose, as it works with tourism providers around the world to combat this horrific, but very real side of tourism.

Cruise liners

Cruising for a bruising in the likes of Croatia, Montenegro, Spain, Italy and, of course, the Caribbean, these floating hotels are starting to create a lot of anchor angst with thousands of people landing in on idyllic islands or tiny towns for a few hours at a time. They contribute little to the local economy and the pollution levels in biodiverse beauty spots are not well documented. Read our *Small ship cruising holidays* for alternatives and also some of the cruising issues that we are concerned about.

Cultural insensitivity

This comes in many forms and, in many ways, is often the most common form of irresponsible tourism. So, dressing appropriately in sacred places, learning a bit of the local language, understanding local customs and respecting people's living spaces are all par for the course in responsible tourism. One of the most common faux pas these days is around photography. Taking pictures and selfies here, there and everywhere. Arriving into a tiny village armed with cameras, but no sense of subtlety or empathy regarding how it might feel to be constantly at the end of a lens that has been stuck in our face. Treating people as objects for your entertainment, unless an event has been created specifically for that purpose, is wrong. You wouldn't take a photo of a stranger's child back home and then post it all over the Internet – so why do this with a child overseas?

The other most common issue is anti-social behaviour. Drinking binges, inappropriate dress and anti-social behaviour are just as as common and upsetting in Magaluf as in Malaysia. The easy question to ask is – would you be comfortable with someone doing this in your home? Because responsible tourism recognises that, first and foremost, when you travel, you are entering someone's home. So you need to learn the house rules and just be nice.

Exploiting children

From giving sweets to begging children to visiting orphanages as part of your holiday, the exploitation of children in tourism is a very difficult area. We now have guidelines to holiday companies that offer volunteering trips, with particular reference to working with vulnerable children in any of the following settings: Orphanages; children's homes; youth centres (including drop-in centres); residential facilities; trafficking shelters; women and children violence refuges and other similar settings.

Irresponsible hiking and biking

In general, hikers and bikers are pretty switched on to conservation issues, but adrenaline addiction rather than adventure in remote places has become a new trend, often making the expeditions more about the achievement than the journey. The charity climb epidemic is spreading throughout the world now, with thousands landing on the hills, trampling and littering, with little financial benefit for local people and

huge environmental destruction. Some charity companies or race organisers have responsible tourism policies, but they are rare. Charity and competition is good, churning up a precious landscape, not so much.

Similarly, mountain biking is a huge growth area in many destinations. Many are switched on to the potential negative impacts of frightening not only wildlife but other trail users, such as hikers and horses, but also to the damage caused to the landscape by braking hard or skidding. But, many are unaware and don't want to think or see beyond their next bend or bump. Responsible tourism destinations need to work together in partnership between governments, national parks, state parks and walking or biking groups, to create the right guidelines and messages for all lovers of the outdoors.

Irresponsible wildlife watching

There are good ways and bad ways of doing most things, but responsible wildlife watching is thankfully on the up. However, there are still guides, drivers and tourists who will break all the rules just to get the right shot to put on Facebook, up close and personal with a tiger or hugging a dolphin. In fact any hugging, petting or walking with wild animals is not only irresponsible tourism, it is just wrong, and you should stay clear of it. Each of our wildlife-watching holidays comes with its responsible rules and regulations, and you can see them all by visiting our website.

Shark cage diving

Shark cage diving is big in South Africa, and many claim it is responsible for the increase in great white shark attacks. This is because very often the sharks are attracted artificially to the site by throwing chum (dead fish, offal and blood) into the water. Attracting wild animals in this artificial way can never be responsible in our view, as it disrupts natural behaviour. There are some responsible diving companies, however, which do not use chum, so the shark viewing becomes no more harmful than any other kind of wildlife safari. So if putting yourself into a cage and surrounding yourself with sharks is your thing, always ask your operator if chum is used, to ensure your tour is not harming wildlife or people.

⇨ The above information is reprinted with kind permission from Responsible Travel. Please visit www.responsibletravel.com for further information.

Leave no trace: how to travel responsibly

By Oliver Haenlein

A more sustainable tourism industry is imperative for the planet's future health. As it stands, we are depleting the very resources we promote. Irresponsible tourism is damaging both natural resources and social systems, while air travel and energy and water usage have a large footprint.

Dr Sonya Graci, director of sustainability solutions business, Accommodating Green, told Salt: "Tourism cannot sustain itself in its current form for much longer. Destinations are losing the resources people are attracted to; beaches are disappearing, wildlife is dying, the oceans are becoming barren. The status quo cannot be sustained.

"The impact of travel on the social, environmental and economic aspects of a community can be extremely detrimental: 15,000 cubic metres of water would typically supply 100 rural farmers for three years or 100 urban families for two years, and yet the same amount only provides 100 luxury hotel guests with water for less than two months."

However, there are now hundreds of examples of travel organisations leading the way in providing more sustainable options for tourists, and we can also expect national standards and certification, as well as increased political work, to start driving tourism in the right direction.

As individuals, we can also play a role. We can all make a huge difference if we plan our trips responsibly, creating more demand for sustainable projects that produce win-win situations. So take a look below at Salt's guide to responsible travel:

Do:

⇨ Look at providers' and hotels' sustainability and environmental policies before booking. Support the responsible ones.

⇨ Use social media to share positive experiences of sustainable organisations

⇨ Think about your water usage; direct water use in hotels ranges from 100 to 2,000 litres per guest, per day

- Learn about the communities and environment you are visiting
- Respect cultural differences and dress appropriately
- Use local transport or rent a hybrid or electric car
- Support local economies by buying handmade souvenirs and eating in neighbourhood restaurants
- Reduce your energy consumption. Turn off lights and appliances if you're not using them. Don't use too many towels. Put a jumper on instead of turning up the thermostat.
- When buying food, buy produce that's been sourced locally to reduce food miles
- Fly less or offset your flight if you have to. Fly direct to help reduce emissions

Don't:

- Drop litter; carry your own reusable shopping bag so you don't contribute to the plastics problem, and refill water containers rather than buying bottles
- Stay silent if you're concerned about a business' environmental impact. Complain and tell people about it.
- Feed wild animals, pick plants or wild flowers
- Buy drugs or engage in sex tourism
- Buy products derived from endangered or protected species
- Foster a begging economy by giving presents or money to local children
- Take pictures without first asking for permission

- Let bargaining become a sport – pay a fair price that both of you are happy with
- Rely on foreign-run establishments, tours or activity companies
- Think that everyone is there to serve you, even if many people's livelihoods depend on tourism
- Take part in sports or activities that damage the natural environment, for example dune buggy driving.

2 July 2015

- The above information is reprinted with kind permission from Salt. Please visit www. wearesalt.org for further information.

Are travel philanthropists doing more harm than good?

An article from The Conversation.

THE CONVERSATION

By Marina Novelli, Reader and International Consultant in Tourism and International Development, University of Brighton

It seems like the best of both worlds. People using their hard-earned vacation time to give something back to those worse off than themselves. At its finest, travel philanthropy is seen as a form of direct development assistance – a benign initiative flowing from the travel industry and travellers into conservation initiatives, community projects and philanthropic organisations.

As Nobel laureate Wangari Maathai commented at a conference in Tanzania in 2008:

"Travel philanthropy was born out of the frustration with conventional aid and ineffective philanthropic giving, as a form of development assistance flowing from the travel industry and travellers directly into conservation initiatives, community projects and philanthropic organisations."

The notion that one can 'do good' by 'giving back' while engaging in leisure or travel is an extremely attractive proposition. However, the reality is that we often fail miserably to fully understand our role as individuals travelling into unknown lands.

Guilt-edged

Philanthropy has shifted from being the preserve of the rich and famous to one of ordinary citizens interested in sharing their more modest wealth. Springing from the consequent democratisation of charitable gift-giving and from the growth of international travel and tourism, travel philanthropy is embedded into an increasing worry, or we might say 'guilt', about the socio-economic welfare of those living in less-privileged conditions around the world. So how can we ensure the

intention to do good while travelling has a positive outcome?

In my research into the ways in which different types of travel philanthropy can facilitate mutually beneficial exchanges between hosts and guests, I have found that it is a growing niche within the broader field of philanthropy. My research in 15 countries in sub-Saharan Africa has highlighted that it can share much with strategic, social entrepreneurship and social justice philanthropy, but can also exhibit tonalities of traditional philanthropy, at times leading to dependency and other related sustainability issues.

The giving of time and money can be the core purpose of the tourism experience, such as in conservation holidays. It can also be an incidental consequence of travelling to locations affected by poverty or major health and environmental problems; a tourist might be inspired to sponsor a school place or decide to assist communities affected by HIV/AIDS, or species in danger of extinction.

Geography of compassion

Tourism has somehow become a vehicle to channel acts of giving between international visitors, who perceive themselves as being more fortunate than others, and those who live in more precarious conditions.

However, there are doubts about whether travel philanthropy actually translates into effective and equitable development, or whether its expansion has caused what Mary Mostafanezhad from New Zealand's University of Otago calls a "geography of compassion", with associated problems of aid dependency, a worsened poverty cycle and delivering ambiguous evidence on its sustainability and impacts.

Clearly, there is a risk that even the most well-intentioned traveller can end up doing more harm than good.

Problems exist when the goal of altruism, the pursuit of individual gain and the desire for social status become blurred motivators behind the act of giving and volunteering. The boom of so-called orphanage tourism is a disturbing example, criticised for promoting voyeurism and encouraging unscrupulous practices.

There is a warning in the idea of 'voluntourism' which since the 1980s has sent individuals with particular skills to volunteer in developing countries. It has proved so popular that it has ballooned into a commercial tourism product in its own right, now worth about $2 billion annually. Every year, armies of westerners – usually young and white – descend on countries in Africa and Asia and tour operators often end up manufacturing work for these volunteers to do.

Facebook fodder

While it allows the participant to beef up their résumés – or add a feel-good photo to their Facebook profile – it doesn't necessarily mean they're making any meaningful difference to the local community.

I recall visiting newly built schools funded by well-intentioned philanthropists who had visited remote rural villages in Namibia, Tanzania and Swaziland. They were turned into empty shells with no teachers as the local government could not afford to employ qualified teachers, or relying on the service of unqualified volunteers from the West. Worse still, I saw schools being painted every two to three weeks at the arrival of a new batch of willing volunteers.

In the view of such criticism, identifying and implementing sustainable forms of travel philanthropy can be challenging, but not impossible.

Amy Scarth, an expert in tourism and international development and director of volunteer tourism firm Big Beyond, urges people to leave the 'honourable' tourists alone and focus any criticisms on careless organisations. She argues that it is no crime for the volunteers to get something out of the experience themselves, but she also calls for a focus on longer-term 'human impact' that reduces the need for external support, rather than a short-term cash injection.

The University of Brighton is involved with projects such as the Peer2Peer Capacity Building in Tourism students' initiative in The Gambia which seeks to move away from traditional philanthropy and make the process more about an equal exchange of knowledge than about the givers and recipients of largesse.

Local participants get training in niche tourism product enhancement, business planning and entrepreneurship development, while those visiting benefit from local knowledge, indispensable for the completion of their final-year project work at the university. For a change, power relations are shifted, whereby those 'helping' are not just those visiting, but those visited. It is a 'trade-plus-aid' form of philanthropy where participants offer far more than just fees for their travel and accommodation, and follow fair trade principles and practices.

Travel philanthropy can be an unpredictable form of giving. There are clear risks of inappropriate practices and interrupted projects. What we have learnt is that if philanthropy is to benefit local communities in developing destinations, it should have a long-term plan agreed and implemented in partnership with local players. And it should provide what the community (not the donor) wants and needs. Lastly, it should aim to become sustainable, whether it focusses on an individual scholarship, aims to help a broader community through school or clinic infrastructure, or is a combination of the two.

27 July 2015

⇨ The above information is reprinted with kind permission from *The Conversation*. Please visit www. theconversation.com for further information.

The future of travel: what will holidays look like in 2024?

By Will Coldwell

Hotels on the moon, hologram staff, danger-zone tourism... this is how our holidays will look in 2024, or so says a new report. But we've got our own ideas – and would like to hear yours, too

What does the future hold for travel? Check-in by robot? Budget space flights? Virtual holidays? Flight comparison site Skyscanner is offering a glimpse of what the 2024 holiday experience could be like with its *Future of Travel* report. We've digested the findings and come up with a few ideas that we think would benefit the world of travel. But what would you like to see in future?

Hotel room of the future

They say: Within ten years travellers will "have no need to encounter a single human being" from the moment they check in. Instead, hotel rooms will be transformed into digital, hyper-interactive spaces in which even the pillows will be "embedded" with electronics to massage your neck and wake you up in the morning. The walls will display high-definition images of your friends and family, hologram personal trainers will hang out with you and the shower will use sound technology to "agitate" dirt from your body, using a traffic light system to indicate when you're clean enough to get out.

We say: Thanks shower, but we're doing just fine when it comes to washing ourselves. As for the prospect of photographs of our friends and family glaring down at us from the walls, surely this will only serve to hammer home just how isolated one feels trapped in a computer-dominated digi-limbo, with a better-looking-than-you hologram making you feel insecure about those profiterole-shaped bulges around your waistline. Meanwhile, it's only been one night and your partner has already realised they can get better pillow talk from the, well, pillow. You've never felt so alone.

In a nutshell: Computer says: "You're dirty."

Space travel

They say: For the ultimate in "corious traveller bragging rights", how about a brief time spent floating weightlessly in low Earth orbit? It's something that should become relatively affordable (i.e. $75,000) compared to the cost of, say, an actual Apollo-style excursion to the Moon. That said, architects Foster +

Partners are currently involved in a project with the European Space Agency exploring ways they could build structures on the Moon with the help of 3D printers, so a lunar hotel could be on the horizon.

We say: It's bad enough having to listen to someone recounting the time they befriended a local harem pants salesman during their gap year in India, let alone the time they accidentally sneezed in their own face while experiencing zero gravity. A moon colony, however, does pique our interest.

In a nutshell: Get saving.

Underwater experiences

They say: Sub-aquatic hotels will be a "far more mainstream proposition" by 2024 and underwater tourism will certainly trump space travel. As Skyscanner CEO Gareth William says: "I suspect you would get more from it, because there is more to see down there than in space." That said, the Poseidon Underwater Resort in Fiji, which was due to open in 2008, is still nowhere near ready.

We say: It may not cost as much as space but sleeping with the fishes is still going to be beyond the budget of 99% of holidaymakers – when it does finally open, a week at the Poseidon resort in Fiji will cost £9,000.

In a nutshell: Don't hold your breath.

Local travel

They say: Peer-to-peer collaboration will take over the world, and within the next decade between 5–10% of people could be renting out their homes to travellers. Increasingly, 'social travel' – from accommodation to supper clubs and other experiences – will become part of the traditional travel industry. New tools will lead to collaboration between tourists and people in the destinations, helping create more localised and personal travel.

We say: As personal, authentic experiences go mainstream, what next for the current set of supper-clubbing, airbnbing globetrotters who like to think of themselves as travellers not tourists? The only way they will be able to distance themselves from the travelling masses muscling in on their territory is to drop the idea of social travel altogether (so 2014) and instead adopt an anti-social approach: the countryside will be awash with hipsters being mindful – alone – in the woods.

In a nutshell: Forget secret supper clubs – expect secret holidays.

Extreme travel

They say: In the further pursuit of 'bragging rights', tourists will start pursuing adventures in extreme destinations. Travellers will want to be the first to drop in on so-called 'forbidden zones', destinations once rendered inaccessible by conflict or political instability or, conversely, be among the last people to see a habitat or species threatened with extinction. Lebanon will become the new Dubai, Angola could take off too, and the chance to spot a bare-faced tamarin before the species dies out will be a lifetime holiday highlight for a lucky few.

We say: Firstly, anyone who goes on holiday for 'bragging rights' is an idiot. As for travelling to forbidden zones, fine if you've got a genuine interest – but even then let the story of Matthew Miller, the American who wanted to secretly investigate the human rights situation in North Korean prisons – and is now experiencing them at first hand – be a cautionary tale.

In a nutshell: Don't do it.

Five things we'd like to see in 2024

Airships, the return of

Ever since the Hindenberg disaster, the idea of travelling beneath a huge balloon of highly inflammable gas has – perhaps understandably – been on the back burner. But now they are back in development: safe, environmentally friendly and with the potential to stay in the air for weeks at a time, dirigible transportation seems to us like the closest we'll come to living in the clouds.

Transatlantic trains

London King's Cross to New York's Grand Central without changing trains? Someone needs to start digging that tunnel.

Virtual reality destination testing

In the future, holidays from hell should become inconceivable. One way of ensuring this is through virtual reality destination testing. Simply pop on

an Oculus Rift headset and go for a stroll. Mould in the hotel room? Building work in the pool? Then go somewhere else or sort out the problem before you go. Never again shall unsuspecting holidaymakers be faced with such imperfections on arrival.

Multi-lingual brain implants

"Me... Want... Beer?" In the future, the linguistic ineptitude of British travellers will be an irrelevance thanks to the invention of multi-lingual brain implants that you can inject into your skull at all good chemists. The result will be perfect fluency in every language of the world, meaning you can buy souvenirs, argue with taxi drivers and, yes, order a beer, wherever you go.

Insta-hols brain zaps

(Probably) using the same technology of multilingual brain implants, in the future you won't even need to go on holiday to get that refreshed and relaxed feeling.

Instead, just zap yourself with a 'holi-rod' and be transported to your destination of choice. Two minutes later you'll be back in the office, this time with a brain full of wonderful memories, such as the delicious cocktails you drank in that underwater hotel, and how clean you feel from the intelligent shower you had that morning. Mega bragging rights indeed.

29 September 2014

⇨ The above information is reprinted with kind permission from *The Guardian*. Please visit www.theguardian.com for further information.

Google Streetview – sightseeing from your own home

Maybe you're short on cash? Scared of flying? Or just quite fond of sitting at home eating chocolate in your onesie? Once upon a time, these afflictions would have left you stranded – unable to keep up with your trendy friends who spent the summer trekking around famous landmarks in a hot and sunny climate. But not any more! Now, thanks to the power of the Internet – and Google Street View – you can tour the famous sites you've always wanted to see, without ever leaving the comfort of your own sofa.

Here are our top nine 'must see' Street View locations:

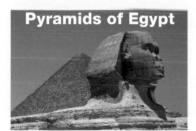
Pyramids of Egypt

The Great Barrier Reef

The Taj Mahal

Stonehenge

The Grand Canyon

Venice

Angkor Wat

Galapagos Islands

The Northern Lights

If there is a future for Space Tourism then what are its impacts?

The very unfortunate Virgin Galactic SpaceShipTwo accident last weekend has prompted a debate about the value of Space Tourism – whether it will only ever be the reserve of the super elites or whether Virgin Galactic is just the beginning of the next stage in civil aviation.

There are those that hail Richard Branson as this era's Orville or Wilbur Wright, a pioneering aviator expanding horizons for the future of aviation. If this is the case, then what is its future?

The immediate future for Space Tourism is essentially civil aviation at a very high altitude, offering passengers with a few moments of zero gravity. Those customers will be the elite of the elites if tickets are going to cost anything like $250,000.

Yet, if the Department for Transport is willing to spend time (and they never seem to have time to do anything we ask of them) carrying out a public consultation on the possible locations of future spaceports then there must be some future for the industry.

What would be the implications of a growing Space Tourism industry?

There would be significant safety considerations, which we raised back in 2007. If the Space Tourism industry does grow then these safety concerns will need greater attention.

There are also going to be implications for the environment, particularly the climate. Richard Branson claims that the CO_2 emissions involved with putting a space tourist in orbit for around a minute would be similar to the emissions associated with an economy round trip from London to Singapore. There are also concerns about the impact on the climate of soot emissions at extremely high altitudes, which could dwarf the non-CO_2 impacts associated with today's civil aviation.

The small number of passengers that could be carried on a Virgin Galactic SpaceShipTwo means that the individual climate footprint of each space tourist is likely to be huge. If passengers reach a few thousand a year within ten years, as Simon Calder suggests, then there would be an increasingly significant impact on the climate.

For today's aviation industry, there is already a gap between technological innovation and growth in emissions. If Space Tourism does become a growing part of the industry then that gap will become even greater.

Richard Branson is one of the biggest supporters of Space Tourism. Yet, he also pledged to commit $3 billion to tackle climate change in 2006 and has so far only delivered a tenth of it. For the future of the Space Tourism industry, and indeed civil aviation as a whole, Branson needs to think about and invest far more in the technology that would be needed to deliver it without damaging the environment.

5 November 2014

⇨ The above information is reprinted with kind permission from the Aviation Environment Federation. Please visit www.aef.org.uk for further information.

© Aviation Environment Federation 2015

Hotel staffed by humanoid robots set to open in Japan this summer

By Anthony Cuthbertson

The world's first hotel staffed entirely by robots is set to open in Japan later this year, promoted with the slogan "a commitment for evolution".

The Henn-na Hotel will open in the Huis Ten Bosch theme park in Nagasaki Prefecture in July with the hope that by employing "actroid androids" – robots that mimic humans – it will be able to significantly reduce costs.

10 robots will staff the 72-room hotel, capable of cleaning rooms, transporting luggage and greeting guests at the hotel's reception. Rooms will range in price from ¥7,000 (£39) to ¥14,000 (£77).

"We will make the most efficient hotel in the world," said Hideo Sawada, president of Huis Ten Bosch, according to *The Japan Times*. "In the future, we'd like to have more than 90% of hotel services operated by robots."

The humanoid robots will be able to speak fluent Japanese, Chinese, Korean and English, and will have human characteristics such as breathing, blinking and making eye contact.

Other unique features of the hotel include replacing room keys with facial-recognition software and selling rooms through a bidding system.

'Robot revolution'

It is the latest in a wave of automation taking place in Japan and news of it opening follows an announcement by Japan's largest bank that it will be trialling a customer-service robot in select branches.

The Nao robot uses cameras to analyse customer's emotions and a microphone to judge their mood by their tone of voice.

Nestle Japan is another company planning to roll out robots into its workforce later this year, introducing the autonomous Pepper to sell coffee machines in up to 1,000 outlets.

The initiatives follow an appeal last year from Japanese Prime Minister Shinzo Abe to invest in "non-human resources" in order to bring about a "robot revolution".

A government report laying out the country's intentions stated: "The government will seek to improve (factory) productivity through the utilisation of robot technology, thereby improving the profitability of companies and helping to raise wages."

9 February 2015

⇨ The above information is reprinted with kind permission from the *International Business Times*. Please visit www.ibtimes.co.uk for further information.

Key facts

- Travel and tourism's direct contribution to world gross domestic product (GDP) and employment in 2014 was US$2.4 trillion (2014 prices) and 105 million jobs, respectively. (page 1)

- 2.1 million new jobs were generated directly in the sector in 2014, and in total 6.1 million new jobs were created as a result of total direct, indirect and induced activity. (page 1)

- 2014 proved to be yet another successful year for the travel and tourism sector off the back of a modestly stronger economic backdrop. World GDP growth increased from 2.3% in 2013 to 2.4% in 2014. The direct GDP contribution of travel and tourism grew by 3.5%, up from 3.4% in 2013. (page 1)

- All major components of travel and tourism recorded growth in 2014, as did all world regions. Business and leisure spending grew by 3.4%, while travel and tourism investment increased by 3.9%. (page 2)

- Visitor exports growth in 2014, in real terms, was fastest in the Middle East and Africa, but slowed in Asia from 8.1% in 2013 to 4.4% in 2014. Political instability and the declaration of martial law in Thailand was a major explanatory factor for South East Asia's slowdown. (page 2)

- Domestic travel and tourism spending growth is forecast to rise from 3.1% in 2014 to 3.7% in 2015, with global travel and tourism investment also rising from 3.9% to 4.8%. But world visitor exports growth is forecast to temporarily slow in 2015 from 4.1% to 2.8%, before returning to growth of +4% in 2016 and beyond and outpacing domestic spending growth. (page 3)

- Every year, on 27 September, the global tourism community celebrates World Tourism Day. (page 4)

- Reasons for travel are manifold and not restricted to holidays, which makes up only 47% of all domestic trips in Australia. Other reasons include participation in sport events, visiting a friend or relative, or business meetings. (page 4)

- According to the World Tourism Barometer there were over 1.1 billion international tourist arrivals in 2014. (page 6)

- According to 2014 data from the World Travel & Tourism Council (WTTC), nine of the ten countries that rely most heavily on tourism are islands, including the Maldives and the Seychelles in the Indian Ocean, the British Virgin Islands, the Bahamas, Aruba and Anguilla in the Caribbean. (page 7)

- Scandinavia is the world's most well-travelled region with Finland, Sweden, Denmark and Norway all being in the top five. (page 8)

- The average American takes 6.7 trips a year. The large majority of these are domestic trips, making the US the largest domestic tourism market in the world in volume terms. (page 8)

- There is some evidence to suggest that UK residents changed their travel behaviour during the years of the economic downturn in 2008–09, by choosing to take holidays within Great Britain rather than abroad. (page 13)

- Negative impacts from tourism occur when the level of visitor use is greater than the environment's ability to cope with this use within the acceptable limits of change. (page 16)

- An average golf course in a tropical country such as Thailand needs 1,500kg of chemical fertilisers, pesticides and herbicides per year and uses as much water as 60,000 rural villagers. (page 16)

- Australians love to travel. About nine million Australians travelled overseas last year, 60% of them on holiday. (page 20)

- Between 1994 and 2012, there was a 28.7% decrease in the number of visitors to national parks in Canada, which may have contributed to the government's 2012 decision to cut budget and staff to national parks. (page 24)

- Sea turtles have been around for millions of years. They migrate long distances around the world, feeding on anything from jellyfish to sea urchins and sea grasses, but always return to the same beach they were born on to lay their eggs. The female crawls ashore to lay up to 120 eggs, covers up the nest with sand using her flippers and returns to the sea, never to see her hatchlings. (page 26)

- According to UN Water, 783 million people do not have access to clean water and almost 2.5 billion do not have access to adequate sanitation. Six to eight million people die annually from the consequences of disasters and water-related diseases. (page 29)

Alternative tourism

Any form of tourism that differs from the 'mass market': for example, tornado chasing, couch surfing or visiting sites of natural disasters, as opposed to beach or package holidays.

Domestic tourism

Residents holidaying within their own country, for example Britons who holiday in Cornwall.

Ecotourism

Ecotourism is closely related to 'responsible tourism' and generally refers to a form of travel that is conscious of preserving both the ecology and the local culture/ community of a tourist destination.

Glamping

Glamping refers to up-market, 'glamorous' camping.

Global footprint

A person's global footprint refers to the impact that they have on the planet and the people around them, taking into account how much land and water each person needs to sustain their lifestyle.

Green tourism

The concept of green tourism is very similar to 'ecotourism'. Green tourism involves thinking about how you reach your destination (for example, taking public transport instead of driving) as well as the impact you have on the local environment once you arrive.

Gross Domestic Product (GDP)

The total value of the goods and services produced in a country within a year. This figure is used as a measure of a country's economic performance.

Homestay

A homestay is a form of travel accommodation in which tourists pay to live with a local family instead of staying in a hotel. This form of accommodation is considered to be extremely eco-friendly, and is often used by volunteer programmes. Meals are often included.

Philanthropy

The concept of helping other human beings in an outward looking, altruistic way, usually in the form of a charitable donation of money or property towards an institution that would benefit from help.

Poverty tourism

Poverty tourism refers to the practice of visiting extremely poor areas or communities in search of an 'authentic' experience. Poverty tourism often involves 'slum tours', in which tourists are led around sites such as the Favellas of Rio di Janeiro or taken to visit the street children of Delhi.

Staycation

A home-based vacation.

Sustainable tourism

Sustainable tourism is closely linked to ecotourism and involves having as little impact as possible on local ecosystems and communities when visiting a destination. Sustainable tourists may choose to travel by rail instead of air, for example, and support local businesses instead of international companies.

Responsible tourism

Responsible tourism has minimal social and environmental impacts. It is also beneficial to local communities.

Voluntourism

Tourism which includes volunteer work as part of the tour or holiday experience. This is becoming increasingly popular, especially with gap year travellers. Examples include teaching English to children or carrying out environmental projects.

Assignments

Brainstorming

⇨ In small groups, brainstorm what you know about tourism:

- What is tourism?
- Why do tourists visit the UK?
- Why do people go abroad?

Research

⇨ Conduct a survey amongst your classmates to find out what kind of holidays people go on. You should ask at least five questions and write a report summarising your results. You should also include graphs.

⇨ Read the article *Is it really cheaper to go on holiday abroad than stay in Britain?* on page 14. Now conduct your own research: choose a holiday (for example a city break, a camping trip, or a holiday rental) and find out how much it would cost to take that holiday in the UK and how much it would cost to take your holiday elsewhere in Europe. Create a table to demonstrate the costs for each holiday and share your results with your class.

⇨ Choose a destination in a different continent and research eco-friendly accommodation options. Write down as many options as you can find and feedback to your class.

⇨ Research volunteer-based holidays in a destination of your choice. Design a poster to highlight the different options you find, or create a presentation to share with your class.

Design

⇨ Choose one of the articles from this book and create your own illustration to accompany it.

⇨ Create a travel brochure for your local town that will include suggestions of activities, places to visit and accommodation options.

⇨ Design a poster that will encourage people to take holidays at the British seaside.

⇨ Imagine you work for a travel agency and have been asked to create a television advert that will promote 'space travel' as the next 'big thing'. In pairs or small groups, plan your advert and create a storyboard to demonstrate how it would work.

⇨ Design an app that might be useful for tourists.

⇨ Crate a design for a 'hotel of the future' – be creative, it could be located underwater, in space or underground!

⇨ Imagine you work for a charity that promotes green travel. Design a campaign to raise awareness amongst young adults. Your campaign could include posters, TV adverts, radio adverts , social media marketing or website banners. Work ins mall groups.

Oral

⇨ Create a PowerPoint presentation that will inform your school about what it means to be a responsible tourist.

⇨ In pairs, discuss the positive and negative effects tourism can have on a community or destination. Write down your ideas and share with the rest of your class.

⇨ 'There's no need to travel anymore. It's quicker, cheaper and easier to just experience places via the Internet, with sites like Google Streetview.' As a class, debate this statement and discuss your opinions.

⇨ Imagine you have a friend or relative who has never been abroad, how would you persuade them to try visiting another country? Role play the exchange in pairs.

Reading/writing

⇨ Write a definition of the term 'staycation'.

⇨ Read *Economic Impact of Travel & Tourism: 2015 Annual Update* on page one. Write a summary for your school newspaper.

⇨ What is responsible tourism? Write 500 words exploring this question.

⇨ Think of a film you have watched that has a strong sense of place and write an essay exploring why the film might encourage people to visit the country or city in which it was set, for example *Eat Pray Love* starring Julia Roberts increased tourism in Ubud, Bali.

⇨ What do you think holidays will look like in 100 years time? Write a blog post exploring this question.

⇨ Read *Who's a tourist? How a culture of travel is changing everyday life* on page four. The theme of World Tourism Day 2015 was about using tourism to develop communities. Do some research, using this book or the Internet, and find out about a tourism-based project that has been beneficial for its local community. Write a report describing the project and its outcomes.

Acknowledgements

The publisher is grateful for permission to reproduce the material in this book. While every care has been taken to trace and acknowledge copyright, the publisher tenders its apology for any accidental infringement or where copyright has proved untraceable. The publisher would be pleased to come to a suitable arrangement in any such case with the rightful owner.

Images

All images courtesy of iStock, except page 4 © Joshua Earle, page 8 © Dorothy Hübner, page 9 © Kundan Ramisetti, page 13 © Daniel Rozier, page 35 Raining Huang, page 36 Vladim Sherbakof, page 38 © NASA and page 39 Krishnan Shrinivasan.

Images on page 37, from left to right: Aeropixels photography, Sinead Friel, Steve Jurvetson, Gordon Robertson, Ritesh, Cara Acred, Matt Brittaine, Anne Dirkse, Diana Robinson.

Icons on page 5, 10 and 15 are courtesy of Freepik

Illustrations

Don Hatcher: pages 7 & 22. Simon Kneebone: pages 21 & 34. Angelo Madrid: pages 15 & 26.

Additional acknowledgements

Editorial on behalf of Independence Educational Publishers by Cara Acred.

With thanks to the Independence team: Mary Chapman, Sandra Dennis, Christina Hughes, Jackie Staines and Jan Sunderland.

Cara Acred

Cambridge

January 2016